The STORY of PEOPLE

by MAY EDEL

Illustrated by HERBERT DANSKA

LITTLE, BROWN AND COMPANY · BOSTON

The STORY

of PEOPLE

Anthropology for Young People

L70-10012

PZ
1/0
E22

CURR

GN

31.5

.E3

1953

FIRST EDITION

Eighteenth Printing

Published simultaneously
in Canada by McClelland and Stewart Limited

PRINTED IN THE UNITED STATES OF AMERICA

For
Matthew and Deborah

CONTENTS

vii

The STORY of PEOPLE

I.

PAPA FRANZ

ONCE there was a young German scientist named Franz Boas who thought he would like to know more about the color of sea water. Why was it sometimes green and sometimes blue? He wanted particularly to know about the color of the ocean in places where it gets very cold. So one day, nearly seventy years ago, he set out on an expedition. It was only a little expedition, but it was the beginning of something very big and important, something that had nothing at all to do with the color of sea water.

With just one other young man, a friend who had come along to help him, Franz Boas spent a year in an Eskimo village around Hudson's Bay in Canada. For a while he did study the color of sea water. Then he began to find

3

something far more interesting — the Eskimo people themselves.

In those days chemistry, physics and biology had already become important sciences. People knew something about the sun and stars, about chemical elements, about plant bodies and the evolution of animals. But they didn't know very much about themselves. Doctors and physiologists had learned something about the human body and how it works, but the scientific study of man's behavior was just beginning. Very little was known of how and why we feel and think and act as we do. Still less was known in Europe and America about the lives of all the different people in other parts of the world.

Living among the Eskimos, young Franz Boas became very interested in their life and customs. He began to study them seriously. After a while he realized that it was important to gather the same sort of information about all mankind. In this way, he saw, we would find out more about human history, and we would also come to understand people — including ourselves — much better.

WERE THE ESKIMOS SAVAGES?

You have probably read a good deal about the Eskimos and their remarkable inventions — about their snow houses, their sleds and wonderfully trained dog teams, about their harpoons and seal hunts. But these things were not so familiar in Boas's day. He found them very interesting. They made him think about the Eskimo in a new way.

Like most Europeans and Americans at that time, Boas had heard that the Eskimo was an ignorant savage, among the simplest of all mankind. He had no metal tools, no machines, no compasses, not even any matches. He knew nothing at all about modern science. His language was full of sounds that seemed to Europeans peculiar grunts, and he had no writing at all.

A few facts like that do make the Eskimos seem ignorant and savage. But Boas knew that a few facts don't tell a whole story. He realized that the Eskimos were actually very intelligent and resourceful. They lived in a country where there was no wood for houses or fires, where there were few animals to hunt. Berries and greens could be gathered only in the short summer. Yet they managed to keep warm, well-clothed and fairly well-fed. Nobody who was stupid and ignorant could possibly get along in that bleak, difficult country.

Suppose we turn things about for a moment. How comfortable could you make yourself in the frozen northland?

5

Suppose you went out fishing in the Arctic Sea and tipped over in the icy water. Even if you managed to get back into your boat, you would be half-frozen before you could reach land again.

But the Eskimo doesn't worry about this problem. He goes fishing dressed in a watertight fur-lined suit, with warm fur underwear beneath it. And he laces himself right into the skin cover of his fishing boat, so no water can get in. Now, no upset can disturb him. He just rolls over, rights himself, and goes on fishing. (But don't try this trick in *your* canvas kayak. It takes well-trained Eskimo skill!)

6

Or suppose you wanted to light a fire. (Remember there are no matches and very little firewood.)

You probably know the way many people make fires when they have no matches or burning glass or flint and steel. They rub two sticks together. It all seems very simple. Rubbing makes heat, which eventually lights the fine powdered sawdust that comes from the rubbing.

But did you ever actually *try* this? It's a very hard thing to do. Your hands soon get tired, and you rub too slowly to get a spark. If you do make a spark, you breathe too hard on it, and blow it out instead of encouraging it to blaze up.

7

Eskimo working ivory with bow drill

Still, people in many parts of the world have to depend on this way of making a fire. No wonder many of them try to keep fires going all the time, so they won't have to kindle them often.

The Eskimos couldn't keep fires burning all the time. Oil and fat were too precious. So they invented a fire-lighter that worked quickly and easily, a bow drill held upright by the mouth.

ESKIMO INVENTIONS

The Eskimo inventions we have mentioned were certainly very clever. There were many, many others. Some of them were simple.

8

For snow goggles, the Eskimos used strips of wood with just a narrow slit to look through. The goggles cut down the sun's glare and prevented snow-blindness.

When hunters got a big supply of food they sometimes didn't feel like carrying it all home. So they just put it into skin sacks and waited till it froze. Then, using the sacks for toboggans, they could coast home on their dinner.

Perhaps an Eskimo snow house seems like a simple invention, but it isn't really. No other kind of house, not a wooden one or a stone one or a thick tent of animal skins, would be useful in so many ways.

First, there is very little wood in parts of the arctic. If you managed to find enough driftwood for a house, you would have to take it with you when you moved, because you couldn't count on finding any more. And you would have to travel a lot, hunting for food. A stone house couldn't very well be moved at all. If you had a tent, you would have to lug the great frozen skins with you. (Some arctic people in Siberia do just that. They have to sit down and chew the skins each time to make them soft enough to fold or put up again!)

But the Eskimos can certainly find plenty of snow all around them in the wintertime. Two men can put up a small igloo in just a few hours. The only tool they need is a small knife for carving out the blocks of snow. An igloo is warm and sturdy enough to stand up in a blizzard.

A house built of snow sounds cold and dank and drippy, doesn't it? Well, a properly built igloo isn't like that at all. The Eskimos have added many improvements to make their houses warm and cozy.

They have figured out a way of keeping out drafts. They build entrance tunnels to their houses, so that you have to enter the living rooms by crawling through a hole in the floor. Because the living room is higher up, it's warmer. The Eskimos have discovered an important fact — that warm air rises, while the cold air sinks down into the tunnel. They don't know why, but neither did we until quite recently.

Their houses are so snug and warm that they have had to solve another problem. How could they keep the snow roof from melting in on everyone? They've done this by insulation: they simply stretch a skin lining across the igloo to make a ceiling just below the roof. Between this ceiling and the snow roof there is a pocket of air. Since heat doesn't travel easily through an air pocket, the roof of the igloo stays cool and unmelted while the room itself is warm.

Dog Sled

Entrance Tunnel

Animal skins drying

BOAS QUESTIONS

You can see why Franz Boas was impressed by the skill and ingenuity of his Eskimo friends. He began to wonder whether they were indeed so backward as everybody said. Many writers of that day doubted if people like Eskimos could reason or have feelings such as we have.

"Nonsense," said Boas to himself. Of course the Eskimos could think! They couldn't have made all their inventions if they hadn't been able to reason. Only a clever people could have made their living and solved the problems of comfort in so difficult a land. It was true that their way of life was simple, but it certainly was not crude and savage.

In order to find out more, Boas learned the Eskimo language and went to visit in Eskimo homes. There he found that many everyday utensils were beautifully carved and decorated. Eskimo artists liked to make tiny ivory figurines that showed real-life scenes — a moose running, a man driving a dog sled, an entire hunt. And remember, they had no metal tools. Using a bow drill like the one for kindling a fire, but tipped with stone, they could cut through great ivory walrus tusks. And though they had nothing like a compass, they could find their way through

Eskimo hunter's map drawn on sealskin

trackless wastes, and draw accurate maps of any territory they had ever traveled over. These maps too were charmingly drawn.

Again Boas said "nonsense" to the beliefs of his time. People who could create such things certainly had a feeling for beauty just as civilized people have.

Because their language was unfamiliar, and used sounds to which Europeans were not accustomed, it did seem strange at first; but as Boas learned it, he found it had its own exact rules of grammar, and very precise expressions for things that were important to the Eskimo people. There were separate words for falling snow and drifting snow, for melting snow and hard snow, and many different words for different kinds of ice, too — solid ice, melting ice, crumbly ice.

And although they had no writing, the Eskimos had a real literature. They had lots of poems and songs and tales that were handed down by word of mouth, repeated by the old grandparents over and over to eager listeners, till they, too, could hand them on perfectly.

The Eskimos insisted that stories should be told properly. All mistakes were corrected immediately. As a result their reports were very accurate. Boas listened to one story about another European traveler who had visited this Eskimo village a long time ago. Later, he found a report of that visit, written by the traveler himself, a hundred years before Boas's time. And the details as he reported them were exactly as the Eskimos had remembered and repeated them through all those years!

Boas did find peculiar customs, it is true, but wasn't it necessary to examine these and see the reason for them before passing judgment on them? After all, any Eskimo found many European customs equally queer!

14

For example, Eskimos eat raw meat, including many parts of an animal that we reject with disgust. Was this habit just crude and savage? Indeed not. Food scientists have found that the Eskimo diet has a very sensible reason behind it. By eating *all* the animal they manage to be well-fed. Not just choice roasts and chops and perhaps liver — but blood and marrow, brains, fat and even the contents of the stomach; all these give a balanced diet to people who have no milk, cheese, vegetables or eggs.

Since we aren't used to that kind of food, we might not like it. And the Eskimos' disgust, when they first saw strangers eating stale food out of little tin boxes, was just as strong as our feeling about their diet.

Eskimo manners are different from ours too. The Eskimos belch loudly after a meal. But this is not just an impolite habit. To an Eskimo, a belch is a sign that he thanks his host for good food. If he omitted it, he would be rudely suggesting that he hadn't been given enough to eat. So you see, belching isn't *bad* manners in this case, it's just *different* manners.

Do you find this hard to accept? Think of all the changes in styles and manners that have taken place among ourselves over the last few generations! Imagine what your great-grandmother would have thought of the casual "Hi!" by which you greet your friends, or your slouchy way of sitting! Thirty years ago a woman was no lady if she was seen in public without a hat and gloves. All over the world, styles and manners keep changing, and they are full of things that seem strange to an outsider. Are teeth that have been filed to a point any funnier than plucked eyebrows? Is it really more barbarous to hang a ring in your nose, as many people do, than to wear earrings? Isn't it just that we are accustomed to one, and not to the other?

From his study of the Eskimos, Boas came to question many things that were taken for granted in his day. He saw that we had no monopoly on kind and noble thoughts. It is true that his Eskimo friends had no such mastery over nature as did his contemporaries in Europe and America. They did not know how to write, or to build machines to do their work. They had no knowledge of science. In all these ways they were primitive. But Boas saw that this did not mean that all their ways were foolish and savage, while ours were intelligent and good.

There are plenty of crude and savage parts to our own history. The "civilized" British once paid the Indians for every Frenchman's scalp that they brought in. Untold numbers of Africans died of hunger and thirst or suffocation in the slave ships that carried them to a life of bondage in America. And in Boas's own day, children were working up to fourteen hours a day in mills and even in mines. "Spare the rod and spoil the child" was taken very seriously as an educational maxim, and children were frequently beaten with canes or lashes. Such practices would horrify the Eskimos and Indians and many other "savages" who somehow managed to bring up their children without taking such cruel measures. And certainly our grandfathers and great-grandfathers bathed far less often than many of the "primitive" people they looked down upon.

Boas saw that there was a great deal that was good and valuable among the ways of even the simplest and most primitive people, as well as a good deal that could be improved. And he thought this was equally true of us. He began to question the view of "progress" that was popular in his day, that said our ways were the best in all particulars, and that all other people of the world represented earlier and inferior stages of human progress. He wanted to study the way men *really* behave, without taking it for granted that our ways were "good" and those of other people "bad."

Boas had found the Eskimos very intelligent, so surely, he thought, it could not be stupidity that had kept them from making the kind of progress we have in science and invention. Boas wanted to find out what had really happened in history — in our history, and in Eskimo history — to account for the differences.

He began to wonder about human nature itself. He wanted to find out a great deal more about all the peoples of the world. He wondered what made some people kind and generous, others aggressive and warlike. He wanted to find out just how much difference there was in the behavior of the different peoples of the world.

ANTHROPOLOGY BEGINS

Boas asked himself a great many questions, and he knew that the answers could not be found in books.

For one thing, there wasn't even enough information available. Few people had bothered to report carefully on man's ways in far parts of the world. Travelers' accounts were full of yarns to entertain and impress their readers; and you know how easy it is to exaggerate to make a good story a little better.

Most of the people who thought at all about human history sat at home in their armchairs and collected these travelers' tales. They did not usually search for fresh and accurate evidence about the ways of primitive people.

Boas saw that to answer his questions this would not be enough.

First it would be necessary to build up a great body of information about the many different people of the world — not just scattered facts, but full accounts that would show the way they lived together and solved their problems.

And it would not be enough to do what the writers of his day were fond of doing — fit the available bits of information into explanations that seemed reasonable. In science we can't just make up a theory to fit some facts and then think we have proved it because these facts fit. We have to work out ways of *testing* our theories.

Boas wanted to make the study of man into a real science. He decided that scientific knowledge about people was more important and more interesting than the color of sea water. And so, when he came back from the arctic, he began his lifework as one of the pioneers of a new science, ANTHROPOLOGY. Anthropology means "the science or study of man."

Franz Boas settled in the United States. He went on expeditions, worked in museums, wrote many books. But perhaps most important of all, he became a great teacher. He started many of the leaders of anthropology in this country on their careers.

When I became his student, Professor Boas was already an old man. He was known to all of us as "Papa Franz," beloved friend and teacher of most of the leaders and of the teachers themselves. He had lived to see anthropology established as one of the great family of sciences; to know that it had already given valuable help to all the other studies of man, such as history and psychology.

2.

A WORLD-WIDE LABORATORY

WHEN Franz Boas led a research expedition to western Canada, he was one of the pioneers of a new science. He worked on many different kinds of problems. But now that anthropology has become an established science, it has many different branches and there are specialists in every branch, each with a particular skill and interest.

Some specialize in ARCHAEOLOGY, the study of ancient ways. Have you ever found an Indian arrowhead? That is a relic of people of long ago, people who once upon a time lived where you now live. It fell to the ground, and was buried in the earth until you dug it up accidentally.

The archaeologist is interested in finding such traces of people who lived long, long ago. He digs into the earth to look for the remains of buildings, tools, clothing, buried under the accumulated dust of hundreds or thousands of years. Arrowheads, broken bits of pottery, even the remains of garbage dumps give him valuable clues to man's ancient past, clues which he has pieced together into an exciting story of man's gradual mastery over nature.

PHYSICAL ANTHROPOLOGISTS study people and their bones. They measure ancient skeletons and modern children. They want to find out what makes some people tall and others short, whether highbrows are smarter than lowbrows, if redheads really have fierce tempers, and whether there really are any "races of mankind."

Other specialists have gone out to all parts of the world to study the ways and customs of living peoples. They

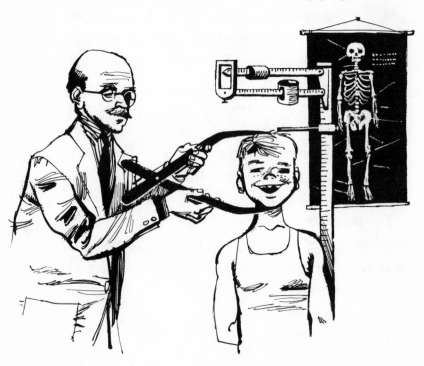

have traveled to Africa and to the South Pacific, to forests and deserts and jungles. It is their job to find out how people lived before the modern world caught up with them, and what happened when it did.

I can give you some idea of how an anthropologist works by telling you of what happened to me. I lived for a year among the Bachiga people, in the highlands of western Uganda, up on top of the middle of the world in the heart of central Africa.

At that time, the Bachiga people were still cut off from the modern world. Although Uganda is a British colony, there were no settlers or traders in this part of it, only a few government officers and missionaries. There were people who had never even seen a European. A few Bachiga, taught by missionaries, had learned to read and write their own language. Some of them had become Christians. But they knew very little of the outside world.

One young man who worked for me was a rare exception. He had traveled with a former employer two hundred and fifty miles to Kampala, the capital city of Uganda. And when he came home even his own family thought he had become a terrible liar, because he told unbelievable tales of buildings with stairs inside them, water that ran from faucets, refrigerators, and shops with unheard-of things for sale.

23

The village of Bufuka, where I lived, still looked as Bachiga villages must have looked for many, many years. The grass-covered dome-shaped huts, with their low, hooded doorways, were grouped in little clusters. Each cluster was surrounded by a hedge that formed a compound in which the cattle were kept at night. The huts were small, smoky and dark, so in good weather everybody worked outside, in the compound and on a kind of hard-packed terrace just beyond the front gate.

I found most of the Bachiga people still dressed in cow- and sheepskin cloaks and skirts. The tiny children went naked, with just a grass band about their waists, and perhaps a string of beads or a bracelet. Men and women alike wore their heads shaved, some with the hair all off, others with short tufts carved into swirling patterns. A few wore a more old-fashioned hair-do — heavy masses of long curls, matted with grease, lengthened with bits of string and decorated with beads and clips. Married women wore hundreds of anklets made of twisted wire.

The Bachiga were farmers. They grew a grain called millet for food, and their cows and sheep supplied them with clothing. They had little use for money, except for the taxes which the British government made them pay. They wanted very few store-bought goods — just soap, sometimes a blanket or two, and lengths of dull-colored

cloth in which the young people liked to drape themselves.

Before I could find out many of the things I wanted
to know about the Bachiga people, I had to learn their
language. Sometimes when you go on an expedition you
can get an interpreter to help you, but I wasn't so lucky.
Only a handful of Bachiga spoke any English at all. In
the beginning I did have one of them for a teacher, but
for the most part I was on my own.

I settled down in a compound my new friends built
for me, right in the center of the village. I had to learn to
find my way around by the little paths that wound up
and down the hills among which the houses nestled.
Bufuka is a little village of about thirty-five adults, so I
got to know all of them — their names, their daily round
of work, their plans and problems. I could attend the two
weddings that took place while I was there, and mourn
with the women at a funeral. I could talk with medicine
men and priests about their work. One of them gave me
a spirit horn to help me on my journey home, with careful instructions about how to feed and tend it.

First of all, though, I had to win their confidence. I was
far stranger to them than they were to me. The children
were scared by the paleness of my skin and my peculiar
colored clothes. They cried and ran away when I came

near. The mothers shared their fears at first. They
snatched up the babies and held them close while I was
around. What was I doing there — alone, apart from the
few other Europeans who lived in the little government
settlement a whole day's walk away? How were they to
be sure I meant them no harm? Perhaps I was a cannibal
or a dangerous witch!

Later on, when I had made many friends, they thought
it was a great joke to look back at these fears and tell me
about them. But in the beginning I had to work very
slowly and carefully. There were even times when *I* was

Author's camp, preparing for safari

a little scared, myself. Late one night during my first weeks there, I heard a great din around my camp. When it turned out to be my household staff and some neighbors banging on my own pots and pans, to drive away a prowling leopard from my tent, I was actually relieved.

My way of working was rather old-fashioned. At that time there were no wire recorders, which anthropologists can now use to bring back legends and stories and even ordinary conversations. I did not even have a movie camera, which is of great scientific use. Movies and recordings make it possible to go over your material many times. Often you notice all sorts of things you hadn't seen or heard the first time. Also, movies make permanent records of things which are very hard to describe in words — dances, facial expressions, or how mothers handle their babies.

Today, groups of workers often go out together and study a particular people. One of them may be a specialist in language, another in art and music, another may be more interested in different kinds of laws or tools. That way the trip is much more interesting for everybody, and the group can find out far more together than they could each discover alone.

Of course, big expeditions with several scientists and modern equipment cost a great deal of money. When I

28

went to Africa, more than fifteen years ago, there still wasn't enough interest in anthropology to persuade people to support many trips such as mine. For the most part workers had to go out alone, as I did. It was in this slow, old-fashioned way that most of our knowledge of the remote peoples of the world was gathered. And, as a matter of fact, a great deal of it is still being done that way. Times are changing so fast that anthropologists can't afford to wait for ideal conditions for their field trips.

Anthropologists are not just interested in "primitive" people. They are interested in *all of mankind* — and we, too, are "people." In recent years they have begun to turn to the study of "civilized" people too. They are trying to find out what makes Americans tick, just as they have tried to find out how Eskimos or East Africans really behave, and why.

In the rest of this book I shall tell you something of all that they have been finding out. They don't as yet have all the answers to all the questions Boas asked; but they now have a great many important clues.

In this book we shall follow some of those clues.

29

3.

PEOPLE ARE DIFFERENT

WHEN anthropologists looked about them at all the different people of the world, they first noticed many, many different ways of living.

There are some people who live in tiny bands in forests or deserts; others live in teeming cities in thickly populated countrysides.

Some people have warrior chiefs, others have priests as chiefs. Some have no chiefs at all. There are vast empires with despotic rulers, and tribes with councils in which everyone has a democratic voice.

There are places in the world where a man may marry many wives; other places where a woman has several husbands; still other people, like ourselves, allow each only one at a time.

We wheel babies about in baby carriages. Some carry them on their backs in little net bags, or strap them onto cradleboards.

There are places where children are independent at the age of twelve; others where they must obey their fathers as long as their fathers are alive; while others — like us — set an age limit for growing up, at fourteen or eighteen or twenty-one, depending on the job, duty or privilege.

The differences between people are not just limited to things like language and government or ideas about children and education. They extend to the most ordinary details of everyday living.

Take a simple matter like sitting down. If you are tired, you will look about for the most comfortable chair you can find — one with cushions and arms; certainly with a back to lean against. But my Bachiga friend Eseri would be very miserable in such a chair! She is relaxed and comfortable sitting on the ground, with both legs stretched straight out in front of her. You try that for a few minutes; you will soon see how the commonest things, the things that seem just to come naturally, are really the results of training and habit.

It's the same with eating, too. Many of us can tell by our empty feeling that lunchtime is near. But Eseri is seldom hungry at noon; the Bachiga eat only twice a day. (On the whole, unless we actually have less food than we need, we don't eat because we're hungry; we feel hungry because it is the usual time we eat.) Eseri has different ideas about what's good to eat, too — not chocolate, nor eggs, nor chicken meat. These all seem disgusting to her. But a freshly toasted locust or a grasshopper would be a welcome special treat. And her manners are different, too. She scoops her food from a common basket with her fingers — but it must be the neatly curved forefinger and the middle finger of her right hand. Being a girl, she eats with the younger members of the family, away from the men. And she never, never tastes sheep or goat meat, although her father and brothers love it.

These great differences are important clues to the anthropologist. They tell him something very important about human nature.

Most animals are born with definite ways of meeting their needs. These ways of behaving are as much a part of them as their hoofs or claws or horns. All cats — house cats, wildcats, lions — crouch silently and pounce upon their prey. Otters on widely separated ponds make identical water-front playgrounds with slippery mud slides. A few models will do for all beaver dams. Each animal behaves like others of its kind. Animals learn something from experience, and from watching their mothers, but this can't be anything very different. Even when an animal does learn something a little new, it has no way of passing on this information or these new ways of doing things to others of its kind.

But man is a somewhat different kind of animal. He is the animal who talks and shares his experiences. He is the animal who learns new ways and teaches them to his children. He has a wide range of possible ways, and he does not follow these untaught. Without training, people cannot make their human way in the world. This human way is a way men have built up for themselves. Because it is man-made, not built into man's body, it can vary greatly. Samoans and American Indians, modern Frenchmen or Russians or people of the Belgian Congo, live in very different ways indeed. To each, no doubt, their own ways seem very natural. All children learn very early to do and think the same things as the grown-ups around them. They start catching on to these things so early and learn so gradually that in many ways they do not seem to have been taught at all — just to have been born that way. And so, to each, their own ways often appear to be "just human nature," while other people's seem strange and unnatural.

There is a tribe in Africa, for example, who knock out their upper front teeth. This is a kind of initiation into being a grown-up member of the tribe. Because they are used to it, they think they look much better that way. And they laugh at their neighbors who don't have the same custom. "Look at them," they say, "with those big front teeth they look just like zebras!"

We are sometimes as prejudiced as that, too. We think our ways are "human nature," and other peoples' different ways less than human. Sometimes we are as mixed up as the child in the Stevenson poem:

> *Little Indian, Sioux or Crow,*
> *Little frosty Eskimo,*
> *Little Turk or Japanee,*
> *O! don't you wish that you were me?*
> . . . .
>
> *You have curious things to eat,*
> *I am fed on proper meat;*
> *You must dwell beyond the foam,*
> *But I am safe and live at home.*

The anthropologist looks at all this differently. He sees that all these ways are HUMAN — otherwise they couldn't happen. They are man's different ways of getting along in the world, of providing food and shelter, peace and security and happiness for himself and his children. Not all ways of life do this equally well, but they must all do it well enough so people can manage to survive.

Anthropologists have a scientific name for the whole body of knowledge and skills, customs and habits, which men have built up and by which they live and work. They call it CULTURE. A people's culture includes all their inventions, all their customs and practices, all the things they believe in — everything they have learned and pass on to their children. It includes government, art, religion, language, the way people make their living and the way they act toward each other; even the way they express their feelings.

To the anthropologist, culture is not a jumble of queer customs. It is a whole way of life people have built up over the hundreds of generations of their history. To understand it, anthropologists have to follow the course of human history, and study the different conditions under which the people of the world have lived.

4.

MAN THE HUNTER

THE story anthropologists have to tell us begins in the very early days of human history.

Usually, history books begin about four or five thousand years ago, in ancient Egypt or Babylon. But man's history is really much longer than that, perhaps as much as fifty times as long.

Man began as a hunter with only the crudest of weapons. He gathered seeds and roots and berries, taking whatever he could find ready to his hand. Slowly he learned to make efficient tools. It is only in the last ten thousand years or so that some men have learned to farm, to put fire and wind and water to work for them, to build cities and skyscrapers.

Archaeologists can tell us a good deal about the early days of human history, but they can't go back to the very beginning. We can imagine our very ancient apelike man ancestors learning to pick up sticks and stones and throw them at their prey, and perhaps piling up brush to make a shelter. But these things made no permanent impression on the present surface of the world. A pebble wouldn't look any different because it had been thrown at a bird. Brush shelters thousands of years old have long since rotted away. Even a fireplace doesn't remain to tell its human tale unless it happens to have been buried over with some long-lasting substance. Without such definite traces of his life, stories about early man must be imagination, not science.

The archaeologist has to begin his account from the time when man *did* leave definite traces of his human activities.

This clear record begins at least 100,000 years ago — perhaps twice that long. It took a long time to convince people that this was so. When, a little more than one hundred years ago, a French archaeologist dug up some flint tools which he claimed were made by man while mammoths still wandered the earth, his fellows scoffed at him. Since that time, a pretty clear record has been traced in stone tools. In the beginning, there were two general types, one in north Europe and Asia, the other in the southern parts of the old world.

Both early types of stone tools were made of flint. They

Digging Stick

Fist Hammer

Hand Axe

Skin Scraper

were designed to be held in the hand. Such a tool could serve many purposes. With it a man could kill an animal, then butcher it, or lop a branch off a tree. Such a tool was quickly made and quickly replaced if it splintered or broke or (luckily for later archaeologists) if it was lost.

There aren't any of these early stone tools in America. Modern scientists tell us that men never came here till a mere 25,000 years ago; to the archaeologist that is only about the day before yesterday!

This is the beginning of the record of human history. The whole of the early period is named after these stone tools, and the slow stages of their development and improvement. This is called the Old Stone Age; but that doesn't really mean that the only material men knew anything about or used was stone. Men certainly knew many other things — how to weave boughs together, perhaps, or sharpen a pointed stick in the fire. But only stone tools could possibly survive to tell their tale.

For tens of thousands of years man's basic tools remained very much the same. Slowly, slight variations were introduced that suited certain tools to different, particular tasks. These more varied tools tell quite a story. For example, one designed as a scraper implies that animal skins were scraped. What a host of ideas that carries with it! Hunting, and skinning the kill instead of just roasting it whole; making clothes, if only a skin cape or blanket to be thrown over the shoulders; planning ahead instead of living from day to day.

About 50,000 years ago man took another very important step forward. At least, that was the date in Europe, where geologists can help archaeologists be much more precise than in some other regions. They figure their dates out in Europe from layers in the earth which were laid down when great rivers of ice — glaciers — moved

39

down over the northern half of Europe. This turned the climate of France and Spain into that of the arctic. Later the ice retreated northward till Europe was as warm as the tropics.

About 50,000 years ago, then, European man first learned to fasten his stone blades to handles. This was a big improvement. It made tools more convenient to handle and, because of the added leverage, much stronger. Tools began to grow far more accurate in style and shape. And the men that made them left other records of their lives as well — scientists have found their hearth fires, and know that they cooked their food. Very conveniently for modern science, they also adopted the practice of burying their dead; whole skeletons have been found, neatly laid out on the floors of caves, with necklaces of beads, and bits of colored clay that were apparently used to paint their bodies.

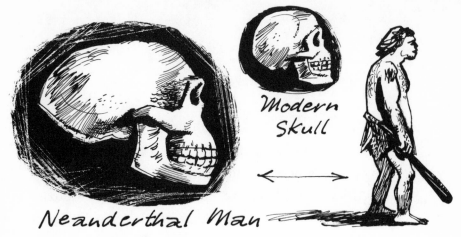

Modern Skull

Neanderthal Man

This habit also tells us something about what men themselves looked like in those days. Before that time, the record of man's own body is just made of little fragments and scraps — part of a skull found in China, a jaw in Germany, and so on. But whole skeletons tell much more. Of course, we don't know what color these people were, nor how hairy, but we do know that they had great beetling brows, and receding foreheads and chins. They certainly didn't look quite the same as we do today. Physical anthropologists call this being NEANDERTHAL MAN. (Don't worry about what Neanderthal means: it's just the name of the place where the first bones of this kind were found.) They haven't quite decided yet whether he belongs on the same branch of the family tree as modern man or not. Perhaps one day your newspaper will carry the story of some startling discovery that will finally settle that question.

41

As time passed, Neanderthal man disappeared in Europe. He was apparently killed off (perhaps even eaten!) by new groups of men, who came into Europe from Africa or the Near East. At that time Europe was once more very cold. The northern part was covered by great glaciers, and no one could live there. The south was more like the arctic than like our present southern Europe. Man found shelter in caves. The mastadon and the woolly rhinoceros and the great saber-toothed tiger were his enemies and his prey.

You have probably heard some very silly myths about the cave man. People speak as if he had been a kind of half-human being dressed in wolfskins, who carried a great knotty club and pulled his wife about by the hair. Our real evidence points to something quite different. Cave men were fully human, not only in their looks, which were quite like modern man's, but in their skills. They had made many complex inventions by this time — harpoons, needles, the bow and arrow, even lamps. Their flint knives and arrow and spear points were evenly balanced, symmetrical, and razor-sharp. They were working in bone, horn and other materials besides stone.

42

And the cave men were artists. They made statuettes in soft stone, and covered the walls and ceilings of caverns with great life-sized paintings, mostly of animals. These are not simply crude outlines. They were the work of skillful artists, experienced, and quite clear about what they were doing.

A very strange thing about these paintings is that they are not to be found on the walls of the outermost caves, the light and airy ones where the men actually lived. They are found deep inside long dark caverns, which can be reached only by crawling through whole series of outer caves and narrow passages. We can merely guess at the reason for this. The guess that seems most likely is that these paintings were not put there for decoration, but to serve some religious function, perhaps that of making the animals whose pictures were drawn there multiply. But this is not the kind of thing we can prove, at least with the knowledge we now have. Archaeology is full of these tantalizing hints; probably it will never be possible to fill in the full record of how earlier men lived — since beliefs, language, and ways of settling quarrels don't leave any concrete record buried in the earth for modern scientists to dig up.

By the time the cave man came to Europe, man's ways of life were already growing different in different parts of the world. During his day, these differences became very clear-cut, as little groups of people lived and worked in isolation. Archaeologists can identify the tools and art styles from those different parts of Europe now and tell them apart. And Asia was even more different. Conquering invaders appeared from there suddenly while the cave men lived in southern Europe. They brought things of entirely new form and style, especially a very efficient new weapon: a spear with a beautifully finished long slender stone head, shaped like a laurel leaf.

44

By 20,000 years ago, men had penetrated to almost all parts of the world except to some of the islands of the Pacific. Some were settled in icy wastes, others in the tropics. Each had to have weapons and shelter and ways of living together suited to the needs of the region where he lived, and the kinds of animals he hunted. Some areas were isolated, cut off by thick forests, or even oceans. In other places, many groups lived in close contact, able to exchange materials and learn from each other. The course of human history was already beginning to grow varied and complicated.

But all these men everywhere, however ingenious or lucky, lived by some form of hunting or fishing. Until very recent times, they all depended on foods and raw materials that they found; it was not until modern times — about ten thousand years ago or less — that any men anywhere learned how to plant seeds and cultivate the soil, or take care of flocks and herds of animals, so as to increase their food supply.

Even today there are many people who are still limited to the more primitive ways of getting their living which were once common to all our ancestors. They hunt and fish and gather wild seeds and roots. They know nothing of farming or keeping flocks and herds. And they do not know how to work in metal. They make stone tools and

45

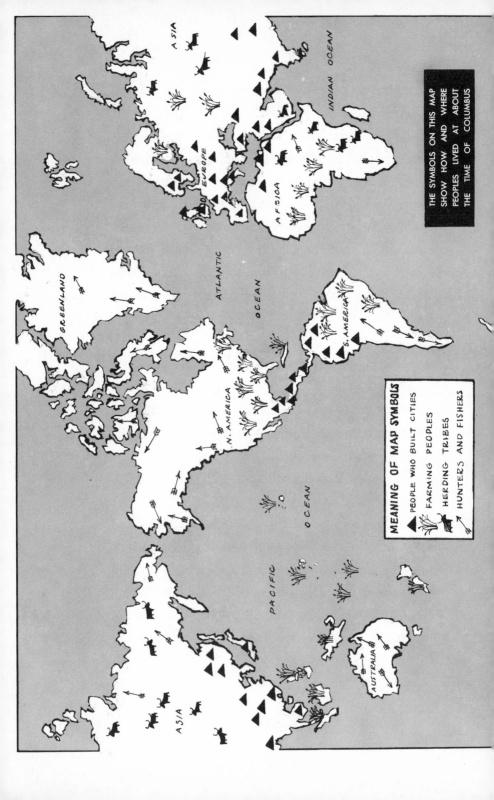

THE SYMBOLS ON THIS MAP
SHOW HOW AND WHERE
PEOPLES LIVED AT ABOUT
THE TIME OF COLUMBUS

MEANING OF MAP SYMBOLS

▲ PEOPLE WHO BUILT CITIES

🌿 FARMING PEOPLES

🐄 HERDING TRIBES

🏹 HUNTERS AND FISHERS

ASIA

INDIAN OCEAN

EUROPE

AFRICA

GREENLAND

ATLANTIC OCEAN

N. AMERICA

S. AMERICA

PACIFIC OCEAN

ASIA

AUSTRALIA

weapons, some of which are quite like those made by Stone Age men in Europe, over ten thousand years ago.

None of these people are unintelligent. They manage to survive and carry on their own traditions in circumstances which are often very difficult and even dangerous. All of them have made ingenious inventions. The Australian has the boomerang and spear thrower, the forest hunter of South America his blowgun. It is he who invented the hammock, far the best sleeping device for tropical jungles. And the Eskimos, as you know, have innumerable brilliant devices to make their arctic living possible.

NEIGHBORS ARE IMPORTANT

But these people have not shared in the progress other people have made over the last few thousand years of human history. Looking at where these people are to be found on a map gives us an important clue to why this is.

You see that for the most part these people live out at the edges of the world, isolated in remote regions. They have made good use of their resources, but they have had only their own limited knowledge and skills on which to build. They have had no neighbors from whom they could learn.

47

Having neighbors has always been important in human history. Those who lived where many different people could come and go have been able to learn a great deal from each other. They were able to share each other's knowledge and experience. When one made a useful invention, the others could learn of it, perhaps improve upon it.

Others were not so fortunate. They lived far away from the accumulating tides of knowledge. The Eskimos, for example, had no neighbors. They shared their wonderful skills and inventions with each other, from Alaska to Greenland. But when they traveled, they met only each other. They met no people who ate different food, wore different clothes, used different weapons, or had very different beliefs. True, there were Indians in the wooded country south of them, whom they ran across from time to time, but these people were nearly as isolated, and had fewer opportunities and skills than they themselves.

The Eskimos were isolated. They could not profit from other people's experience. They could not share in the great inventions men were making in other parts of the world. And this was just as true of the Australians, or the people of the dense jungles in Ceylon, or the desert reaches of South Africa.

Suppose we think of each people's contribution to man's

progress as a little stream of knowledge. When two streams flow together, they make a larger stream. When many of them flow together, they make a great river, which often overflows and sends out little branches in different directions.

There have been many little streams in the world. Some have just flowed along by themselves, without joining any others. Some of these have faded out, or ended in stagnant pools, while others have remained small, sparkling brooks. Still other streams have met to form the great and flowing river we call civilization. We have been lucky enough to live along the shores of this great river. Remote and isolated people, like the Eskimos or the natives of Australia, have not.

Now, let's see what anthropology has to tell us about how the hunting and food-gathering people of the modern world live, how they feed their families, educate their children, and settle their quarrels. At the same time this will give us a little insight into what life may have been like for our own early ancestors.

5.
ESKIMO HUNTERS

WHAT kind of life-ways are possible to hunting people? You already know that the Eskimos were clever hunters, and had excellent clothing and shelter to make life comfortable in the arctic. How did these people live together? What was their whole culture like?

Today many of the Eskimo people have moved into trading centers established by Americans, but the Eskimos of Boas's day — and for many years thereafter — lived in tiny isolated settlements. Their communities had to be small. Even with all the ingenuity and skill we know they had, they just couldn't get enough food for many people to live together in one place.

It's hard to realize how very, very limited Eskimo group living was. An Eskimo boy in his whole life never met as many people as you probably do in one day at school.

But of course, he knew all these people intimately. He knew how many seals each of his neighbors had killed, and who their cousins were married to.

Every tiny Eskimo community had to be entirely independent. No one can possibly afford to travel two hundred miles in a dog sled every time he needs a piece of string, or has to repair a harpoon; so every village just had to supply all its own tools and raw materials. If you were an Eskimo you would know the people of a few other settlements — perhaps someday you might even pack up and go to spend the winter with them — but you couldn't possibly depend on them completely for the necessities of life, or any kind of help.

Even within the community, Eskimo social living was limited by the difficult and dangerous circumstances of life. Everyone in a community was prepared to be helpful, especially in a crisis. All had to be, to survive. But no one could afford to depend absolutely on help from other people. A bad storm, or a long period of bad hunting, could easily wipe out most of a tiny community. One family might find itself all alone, cut off for months at a time from all neighbors. This could even happen to an individual. An Eskimo just had to be completely independent and self-reliant. He had to know how to make all his tools, not just how to use them.

An Eskimo boy in his early teens was a skilled Jack-of-all-trades, able to live successfully a life as isolated as that of Robinson Crusoe. Often, long before he was married, he moved out of his parents' home and built an igloo for himself, supporting himself by his own hunting, and helped out by his young sister, who would sew and cook for him. Naturally, a youngster who was so thoroughly self-supporting had to be treated as a grown-up, responsible person. No one could possibly boss him around.

The Eskimos carried this independence to an extreme. They didn't even have any regular chiefs. If a strong young hunter was also brave and generous, people would look up to him, and might follow his leadership. But he couldn't compel them to. He didn't have any real authority.

All Eskimo ways of living together were based on this background of danger and independence. Marriages were easy to make and unmake: you just walked out on your husband or wife. Lots of Eskimos were married and divorced quite a few times in their lives. People could move to different villages; they didn't have to spend all their lives with one particular set of close relatives. And this pretty well ruled out any very formal law-enforcement. You can't make a man listen when he's two hundred miles away.

52

This doesn't mean that everyone could do just exactly as he pleased. If a man was selfish and lazy, others would be likely to leave him severely alone. If he was too much of a bully, and annoyed other people by his behavior, he would wear out his welcome everywhere, and have nowhere to go. Someone might even quietly knife him one night, with the blessing of everyone else!

Of course, some things that make us need laws and policemen just weren't problems for the Eskimos. Take stealing, for example. Since everyone made his own things, nobody was too poor to have whatever he needed. When times were bad, everyone was hard up. When little food was available, or some special thing was needed by someone other than the owner, it was shared generously. Only young orphans, old people, and cripples were ever seriously worse off than other people. In hard times, they might indeed perish. But when times were fairly good, they would be carried along by the group.

THE DRUM MATCH

The Eskimos did sometimes have terrible fights, and there was nothing official that could be done about that. If official laws had been all, there might not have been any Eskimos left! But they had a way of avoiding such a thing. They had invented ways for people to work off their hard feelings. One of these was the famous drum match.

In a drum match, the two who were quarreling sat opposite each other with all their friends and neighbors about them. Then they took turns playing the drums and making up songs about each other. The tougher the songs were, and the funnier, the worse names they thought up to call each other, the better. The one who could think up the worst and funniest things to sing about his enemy won the contest.

Sometimes a whole village, or two villages, got involved in a quarrel. Then, instead of fighting it out with spears, they might work it out in a tug-of-war. Actually, there was no reason among the Eskimos for real war. When they were told about war by Europeans, they said they didn't understand how people could be so foolish.

55

THE ESKIMOS SHARE THEIR POSSESSIONS

A great deal has been written about the Eskimo attitude toward wealth and possessions. Among the Eskimo people no one tried to get rich. A strong young hunter brought home more food than other people, he had more skins for clothing and boat covers, and he could even marry an extra wife if he wanted to. But this advantage was only slight and temporary. He couldn't store up his extra wealth to use sometime in the future. He couldn't put it aside to buy a television set or provide for his old age. Most of it would spoil, and there wasn't any way of buying and selling. In fact, no one had anything to sell him! And he couldn't use his extra wealth to get any one to work for him. Why should they? They were all perfectly independent, able to make their own tools and go after animals themselves.

The young hunter who brought in more game than other people could best put it to the approved Eskimo use — share it with those of his fellows who happened to be in need at the moment. They wouldn't have to repay him; but he would be laying up a store of good will that would be an excellent provision for himself when he, in turn, was less successful in the hunt.

The Eskimos were thus generous with all their posses-sions. Not only was a successful hunter proud and glad to share his catch; a traveler who found food someone had cached away was welcome to use as much of it as he actu-ally needed, without even asking permission. A man who happened to have extra material — a harpoon or a boat that he wasn't using — would lend it freely to his friends, and never even demand it back unless he really needed it for his own use.

Some people have suggested that the Eskimos carried things too far. They think that the Eskimo habits of shar-ing are just foolish. They say that the Eskimos just didn't have enough foresight to bother about providing for their own future needs, or to care for their belongings, or even to have a clear idea of owning.

This wasn't true at all. The Eskimos were always very careful with all their things. The man who made a tool was its absolute owner. But there was no point in keeping it put away if someone else needed it. That kind of selfish "human nature" hadn't been invented yet. But the Eski-mos were particularly careful about returning lost belong-ings, for they knew that the loss of a tool or a bit of mate-rial might make the difference between life and death to its owner. And they always stored away any extra supplies until they themselves or someone else needed them.

The idea that everyone had a real obligation to the others, and that you could in return count on their sharing with you, was a fundamental Eskimo attitude. It wasn't just generosity. It was a perfectly realistic way of coping with the problem of managing to survive, under their peculiar difficult conditions.

WHO IS BETTER?

You can see that Boas was right in saying that primitive people like the Eskimos had devised many excellent and even admirable ways of living together. It's clear that in the face of their kindness and generosity we can't just feel smug and proud of ourselves.

But we can't say that the Eskimo people are better than we are, either. It is impossible to make that kind of comparison — because our way of living and our problems are very different from theirs. There are millions and millions of us. The things we use are made in large quantities in factories or grown on large farms. You can imagine how mixed-up everything would get if we depended on generosity and kind hearts to see that everyone had enough shoes and ice cream and nuts and bolts!

In order to solve the problem, we have had to invent not only supermarkets and checking accounts, but insurance and unions and social security. Even these aren't doing the whole job well enough. We know that kindness isn't enough to take care of all our problems of special needs like sickness or unemployment. We must keep on trying to work out more efficient ways of guaranteeing more and more people the things they need. When we succeed, we will have achieved much more than the Eskimos can with all their generosity and sharing. For they can only share a little among a few people, while we have the means of producing and sharing abundance for the whole world.

ANGAKOK AND SPIRITS

When Boas began his work, many people thought that primitive people could have no religion. Others thought they did, but that it must be lacking in all noble thoughts, and just be a mass of superstitions.

Anthropologists have found that not only Eskimos, but all people, have religious beliefs and practices. Of course, to any people, other peoples' beliefs may seem like superstition. But the Eskimo beliefs were not all so very different from our own, or from those of such civilized people as the ancient Greeks and Romans. They believed that there was a great and important goddess who was in charge of all the sea mammals who were so important in Eskimo living. And they believed that men had souls, which went to live in a special land of the dead when the men they inhabited died. However, their idea of the soul was a little different from that people nowadays usually hold. They didn't think of a man as having only one soul, but as having many; every part of the body which could be sick or injured had its own separate soul. It could leave the body; and that, in fact, was what was supposed to cause illness.

Eskimo religion, like that of every other people, was not just a mass of curious beliefs and customs. It was a way of trying to get supernatural help when they had problems they couldn't solve. There were three problems that left the Eskimos particularly helpless — bad weather, sickness, and the failure of game animals to appear when and where they should. Eskimo religion was tied up mostly with these things, and it also fitted in with their whole informal way of life. They couldn't afford to have an organized group of priests, any more than they could afford an army or an aristocracy. They did not even have ceremonies and rituals that everybody followed at fixed times and in regular ways.

Instead, every Eskimo believed that certain people, called *angakok,* had special religious powers. Like people

Talking to Spirits

who call themselves spiritualist mediums today, the *anga-kok* were supposed to be able to talk to the spirits and bring messages from them. They were supposed to go to the land of the dead and bring back wandering souls whose absence was causing people to be sick.

The Eskimos also believed that the *angakok* could see strange dark clouds that hung about a hunter who had offended Sedna, the goddess of sea animals. Sedna was a jealous goddess. She would allow none of her animals to be captured by a hunter who had broken any of her special rules. For example, no one was allowed to eat seal meat if he had handled deer meat. He was not even allowed to use the same knife or utensil for both. Sedna insisted on keeping her department of life quite separate.

When a hunter thought he had broken a rule, he went to the *angakok* right away. If he did not do penance, the cloud would spread, and keep everyone from getting food. When luck was bad, people went to an *angakok* to find out if any Eskimo had perhaps broken some rule without realizing it at the time.

MAGIC AND SCIENCE

How was it possible for such intelligent, practical people as Eskimos to have these beliefs? Because we know about modern science, we can see that their ideas did not really explain things. But the Eskimos knew nothing about germs or weather forecasting. They could not make scientific studies of the way in which animals live and migrate. They had simply worked out a set of beliefs that fitted in with the things they did know. Like many of our own ancestors, a few hundred years ago, they could only call unexplained things magic, or the work of spirits.

For example, the explorer Stefansson tells this story. He once showed some Eskimo friends his field glasses. "Oh," they said, "now we can see where distant animals are grazing. Splendid. But where will they be tomorrow when we want to hunt them? Can your glasses show us that?"

"Of course not," Stefansson replied.

"Well, in the next village there is an *angakok* who is much more powerful. He can easily see across mountains and into tomorrow."

And because they had no knowledge of science, they could not see the difference between the real powers of the field glasses and the *angakok's* magic — except that the *angakok* seemed to them more powerful, because he claimed to do more.

Not everyone could be an *angakok*. The *angakok* were people who had epileptic fits. At times they would lose consciousness, jerk and writhe and make strange sounds. By careful training, an *angakok* could learn how to control these fits. He could have such a fit when he was supposed to go into a trance. The writhing and jerking was the sign of his tussling with the spirits, and the strange noises were the voices of the spirits talking through him.

This sounds like some kind of deliberate trickery. But it wasn't at all. The *angakok* was not a trickster. He really believed in his own magic. He told in great detail about the visions he saw during his trances, and these visions were not made up. When a man has fits, psychologists know today that the things that pass through his mind seem very real to him. As the other Eskimos watched the *angakok* writhing and jerking, it was easy for them to imagine that he was wrestling with the spirits they believed in. The peculiar noises he made could be explained as spirits' voices.

Modern doctors also know that people who feel sick can sometimes be helped just by the idea that they are being taken care of. They feel comforted and reassured, and so they feel better. This is probably the reason why the magic of primitive people sometimes worked. The Eskimos believed that the *angakok* could help them. So, if they were sick, he sometimes did make them feel better. If they were starving, he helped them get the extra courage to look a little farther, until they actually did find game to eat.

This is a very brief picture of Eskimo culture. It just gives us some of the highlights. But it does show us how Eskimo customs and beliefs suited the needs of their hunting way of life.

GETTING A LIVING SETS THE STAGE

Eskimo culture is similar in basic ways to what we find among other hunting and food-gathering people, and very different from the far more complicated culture we have developed.

You see, the way man gets his living sets the stage for much of his social living. Getting food and shelter isn't just a matter of using certain tools and skills. It involves people, and their ways of working together.

Our ways of making a living are complicated, and so are our ways of living and working together.

Have you ever watched people building a house? Bulldozers come to clear the site and dig the foundations. A man comes with a cement truck, and goes away again. Totally different people put up the framework. Later on electricians and plumbers, roofers and painters, will finish the job. None of these people are related to the man who is building the house. They are total strangers to him. He hires them to do the particular job.

These are the things you can see going on. There is a lot more behind the scenes that is even more complicated. There are all sorts of deeds and certificates and licenses which are necessary. Inspectors are sent around to see that the wiring is safe and the plumbing sanitary. And after the house is finished, the builder may not even move into it. He may sell it to a total stranger.

These complications are so familiar to us that we don't think about them much. We are used to depending on the work of hundreds of people who never even see each other. We drink milk from distant farms, pasteurized and bottled in a large dairy and brought to our door by a milkman whose whole job is just delivering milk. He collects the money, but he has nothing at all to do with setting the price. We're so used to all these complications that we just take them for granted.

But if you really stop to think about it, you'll see right away that this working-together of many different people needs all sorts of complicated machinery — banks and government regulations and large-scale business enterprises — if it is to work at all. And since our food comes from all corners of the world, it even leads to attempts at world government.

HUNTING LIFE IS SIMPLE

No such complicated arrangements were necessary when the Eskimos had to satisfy their needs for food or shelter. When an Eskimo wanted to build a house, he found the materials for it all about him. He didn't have to import the snow or buy it in a store. He cut it into blocks with a knife he made himself, and no one had to give him permission. He could use the help of a few friends to put it up more quickly, but he could do it all himself if necessary. He didn't need money; he didn't need hired workers; he didn't need any licenses or permits or to organize a work bee or to get skilled help. None of these things had any possible place in his life.

66

The social side of Eskimo work was simple. It involved only a few people, in direct relation with each other. Each individual was basically a separate and independent unit.

The rest of Eskimo social life was simple, too. They had some splendid ways of getting along together, but they were simple, direct ways that suited their needs. They did not include city-planning commissions or chambers of commerce or rotary clubs, to say nothing of marriage-license bureaus or an elected national congress.

All this was equally true of the Australians of the central desert, the forest hunters of Ceylon, or the acorn diggers of our Western mountains. They all lived in tiny communities that were quite independent. They did not depend on trade. They had no specialized craftsmen. Everyone had to be a Jack-of-all-trades, though some might be a little better than others at certain skills. They had no more basis for riches than the Eskimo. There were no rich men and no poor men, no masters or servants among them. Everyone had to work, and among all of them there was a good deal of sharing in the group.

This doesn't mean that the culture of different hunting and food-gathering people was all identical with that of the Eskimos. It couldn't be. Even their inventions had to be different, to suit the very different needs of the different parts of the world where they lived.

The Eskimo hunter, living in the frozen arctic, makes excellent harpoons and knows how to spear seals through ice. These skills would not be of much use to a bushman hunter in the South African desert, who faces a very different challenge. He has learned quite different things — how to stalk game, for example, by mingling with the herd in disguise. He has to provide a water supply to tide himself over dry periods, and he does this very ingeniously. He blows out the contents of ostrich eggs and fills the shells with water. Then he buries them in the sand. When he needs the water, he has only to suck it up through a hollow straw.

Differences in the country people live in, and the knowledge and skills they have, make a big difference to their whole way of living. Some forms of hunting are better pursued singlehanded, others by groups of men. People who live by the banks of rivers or lakes and have learned to fish can live in more settled villages than those who depend on pursuing game. The size of settlements, the nearness of neighbors, may all depend on how much food is available and how well men handle the task of getting it.

Naturally, then, over the many generations of their history different hunting people have built up ways of living

68

together that differ in many ways from those of the Eskimos. Suppose I tell you something about the people of Central Australia, so you will see what these differences are like.

6.

THE DESERT AUSTRALIANS

The inhabitants of Central Australia lived under even more difficult conditions, in some ways, than the Eskimos. Their homeland was almost a desert. Every five or six years it would rain, and a lush green growth would spring up. But most of the time the land was dry and almost bare. The men knew how to hunt, but animals were scarce. It was a great stroke of luck to bag a kangaroo, an emu or a wallaby. While the men hunted for game, their wives and the old people spent all their time foraging for the vegetables and bugs that provided most of the staple food. They had to know everything about every inch of their land to find enough food for the group to survive. They had to know where water was sure to be found during a dry spell, where roots could be dug, when and where there would be insect larvae or seeds that they could harvest; all this in order to survive.

These desert Australians were unbelievably poor. They wore no clothing. Their homes were just open camps, hollow places in the dust by the side of a precious waterhole or, in very bad weather, windbreaks made by weaving a few branches together. Packing presented no problems, when they moved from one camping place to another. A woman just had to pick up her digging stick, her wooden bowl, and a string bag for the food she might find or dig. That was just about all she owned. Her husband, too, could carry all his possessions with him very comfortably. He had only a few weapons, and a little skin bag in

which he kept his valuables — such things as lumps of red and yellow clay (he used these to decorate himself at religious festivals). Since he had to travel a long way to find the clay, it was very precious. Knives, however, were simple to get. If he needed a new one, a man just picked up a stone the right size and quickly chipped it into a shape men have known for tens of thousands of years. He had no bow and arrow — only the ingenious boomerang and spear thrower.

This provided a very different setting from that of the Eskimos, who roamed widely after big game. One particular section of land had no special value to an Eskimo. To the Australian, land was very important. He had to comb and recomb it for every scrap of possible food. No wonder that it was carefully parceled out, with different family groups each having their assigned area to move about in.

A man lived all his life on the piece of land which belonged to his father's family. He and his relatives had exclusive rights to their land. If anyone else trespassed, they would put him to death.

This doesn't mean that different groups were enemies. The reason for the division of the land was to avoid fights, not to start them. Each group had the right to use its own tract without being molested, and they were supposed to respect each other's rights.

The family which lived together permanently on its tract of land, generation after generation, was not a loose informal group like the Eskimo community. Everything about it was covered by strict rules. The hunter had to divide his game among certain relatives — a particular portion to his own father, another to his elder brothers, a third to his father-in-law, a choice part to his grandfather, and so on. There was only a small section left for him. Equally strict rules covered whom he might marry, when he should be initiated in the magic rituals known only to grown-up men, and so on. And each family had a council made up of all its old men, who saw to it that these arrangements were carried out exactly by everyone.

These rules seem very awkward and complicated to us, but they fitted in with the rest of Australian life very well. They made it possible for the group to co-operate smoothly, and to share what little they had. In their hot climate the Australians had not yet worked out a way of storing meat. The actual job of hunting was done by a very tiny group. The meat would go to waste if it were not shared. At the same time, by seeking out relatives to give them meat, the hunter helped to keep the different members of the family in touch with each other.

This method of sharing also helped to keep the older people in the group alive. Among the Eskimos the young and strong had the advantage. For them old people were something of a burden. When an Eskimo was no longer able to support himself, he could stay with his children and expect them to take care of him in good times. But if there wasn't enough food, or if a long and difficult trip was necessary, the old people would feel that they were in the way. They might even endanger the others. And so they were abandoned, or took the initiative and wandered away to die by themselves.

The Australians did not place nearly so much value on strength and skill in hunting. Instead, they came to believe that as a man got older he grew wiser, and that his wisdom should be respected and honored. However, in any group there must be strong reasons for the young men to accept the authority of the older and weaker ones, otherwise they might be tempted to take matters into their own hands. And the Australians did believe they had such reasons — very strong ones. For the old men were the keepers of tribal secrets, the sacred knowledge which was supposed to control the well-being of the whole people.

Australian religion centered around the problem of guaranteeing a food supply. They did not know how to farm or to raise domestic animals. But they thought they had a key that would work. They performed elaborate ceremonies, full of dances and sacrifices and little dramas,

74

Initiation rite in Australia

that dealt with the habits of the animals they hunted.
They thought that if they carried these out properly and
obeyed all their religious laws, the animals would be sure
to multiply. When the food supply was scarce, it was due
to some mistake they had made in the ceremonies; they
had to be more careful next time, and all would be well.

75

These ceremonies weren't a form of prayer; they were more automatic than that. They believed the result *had* to follow, just as surely as you expect a button to ring a bell.

This idea that a ceremony has a direct and automatic effect is a common one in the world. We call it "magic." Among many people, this kind of magic was a regular part of religion. And these magical beliefs and practices still exist in many forms even in modern times.

Among the Australians, it was the old men who performed the most secret and important parts of all the ceremonies. Women weren't allowed to know anything about them, except for a few public festivals. The young men learned them gradually. As men grew older, and were taught more, their authority and importance increased. By the time they reached old age, their every word was respected and followed.

Like any other people, the Australians explained their religious practices by myths which they believed in. In the great days of the remote past, they said, spirits roamed the world. At that time there were no ordinary people in the world, and no animals. Then there came "a time of changing over." The spirits went down into the ground, and left behind them representatives to live in ordinary bodies. Each group of spirits started two lines of descendants — one line was a certain family of people, and one was a particular kind of animal which became their totem.

There is a permanent mysterious connection between each family started by a spirit group and their totemic animal which was started by the same spirit. The family never eats the meat of this particular animal, and they know the religious ceremonies which control it. If you belong to the kangaroo family, for instance, you would never eat kangaroo; but you would perform the ceremonies that cause it to multiply.

So you see that on the basis of their religious beliefs, even members of different families are dependent on each other. If you eat kangaroos, you depend on the family that controls them. Thus all food supplies come from rituals that people perform. It seems that everything in Australian living emphasizes the idea of group living and sharing, just as everything in Eskimo life carries through the idea of independence.

If we visited some of the other people of the world who live by hunting and food gathering we would find still other religious beliefs and other ways of living together. The Andaman Islanders off the coast of India live in little villages, the bushmen of the South African desert in roving bands. Some have definite leaders to hold the group together, others respect and follow individuals with special skills. But whenever their resources are limited, they live in tiny groups, where all men work alike, and share their goods in order to survive. And these limitations no doubt held also for many of the early hunters of the remote past.

7.
WEALTHY FISHERMEN

NOT all hunters and fishers, recently or in the past, were quite so badly off as the Eskimos and the Australians. Some of them lived in places where food and raw materials were much more plentiful. They had time to develop more special skills, to pile up goods for the future, to support some men of wealth and power.

Among such wealthy people were the totem-pole Indians of the Pacific Coast of North America. These Indians lived close to great rivers, where (at least until modern salmon canneries began to interfere) millions and millions of salmon swam upstream every year. This great abundance made it possible for the Indians to have plenty to eat without having to work for it all the time.

They had many ingenious ways of catching salmon. They used fish weirs of various sorts. They went night trapping with nets and torches. They fastened baskets under the waterfalls to catch the salmon who failed to make the jump successfully. The whole community would be organized for fishing at the height of the salmon run, and they could catch and smoke enough fish in a few days to last for the year.

When people don't have to hunt every day for fear of starving, they have time for other things. Although none of the arts and skills of the farming peoples had reached this remote corner — these Indians had no pottery, no true looms, no heavy stone axes — they had special arts and skills of their own. They made beautifully decorated boxes and bowls and spoons. They built enormous seagoing canoes, large enough for twenty men to travel in. They were particularly good at woodworking, building great houses as much as two hundred feet long and forty feet wide. These were made of great planks of cedar, set upright, and roofed over with wooden boards.

All these things were made without metal tools. This doesn't seem possible, but it was. First the Indians brought down huge cedar trees by ringing the trunks with fire. Then they split off planks by hammering wedges in all along the length of the tree. This work had to be done very carefully, so that the planks would split evenly. The canoes were made of single logs, hollowed by fire. Then these dugouts were widened by forcing the sides out with

crosspieces, after filling the hollow with water and heating it with red-hot stones. The outside of the canoe was smoothly adzed, the little marks left by the stone tool forming a neat decorative pattern, and a great carved prow was fastened in front.

Because of their better food supply, these people were able to live together in good-sized villages, with far more varied and complicated social rules than those of the poorer hunters and fishers.

Let's see what their villages looked like. Down near the edge of the water, just off the beach, stood a cluster of three or four houses, huge houses where fifty or more people could live together. In front of each house was a weird and wondrous object, the great carved "totem pole." Perhaps a totem pole looks strange and grotesque to most of us. But these people had seen such carving and painting all their lives. This was the only kind they knew and liked.

You may have heard that totem poles were some sort of idol used in religious ceremonies, but that is not true. They were more like the coats-of-arms which aristocrats in Europe used to carve over their doorways or engrave on silverware. Each of the figures on a totem pole had some meaning. It stood for some important title, some great family connection of the chief who was the owner of the house.

The houses in the village all faced the ocean, along a little boardwalk street. Across the street, overhanging the beach, were wooden platforms. These served to anchor the boats, to unload fish, and also as ceremonial places where rival chiefs of different communities could show off their greatness.

These people could pile up great quantities of valuable and beautiful goods, far more than they needed. The

82

chiefs, as heads of the households, could use the extra wealth produced by the relatives who were members of their households. They used it to show off their greatness by showering each other with enormous gifts — great piles of blankets, valuable ornaments, barrels of oil. The one who gave the most proved his greater wealth, and his higher social standing — even though in doing it he might have given away so much that he had nothing at all left but his reputation! But his relatives were proud if their chief was greater than the chief of another household or village. They would work hard to help pile up the goods needed to maintain this position for him, and to a lesser extent for themselves.

The wealthy chiefs had many special honors and privileges. They could hold slaves and belong to more exclusive clubs than other people. They arranged marriages between their children to obtain greater family honors. They formed a special aristocratic class, but they did work along with everyone else.

All these complications were possible because the Northwest Indians had so much more food, and so many more permanent belongings, than most hunting people. But although they had so many clever inventions, they were only the welling-up of one little separate stream of progress. They were out of touch with developments and inventions in other places. Their own little pool could not grow and spread very much, for their neighbors, less fortunate in their food supply, could share very little in this way of life, nor could they add much to it.

The same thing may have been true of some of the other hunting and fishing people of earlier days. Some of them lived where resources were abundant, and also developed high skills and considerable wealth. But their culture never went on to form the basis of more complicated civilizations. It was not until man became a farmer that he had a really permanent and stable basis for the development of new ways in social living, one which could spread widely among the people of the world.

Let's see now how this development came about and what it meant to man.

8.

MAN THE FARMER

U P to about ten thousand years ago there were, so far as we know, no people anywhere who knew how to grow grains or other plants for food. All men lived by hunting, in the ways we have told, and by gathering roots and berries. Then — about ten thousand years ago — the first cultivated wheat was developed from wild grasses. Some scientists think that this happened in Palestine, others in Central Asia. In both places there are wild grasses with the appropriate kind of seeds.

We don't know now just what made the conditions right for this tremendous event at that time and place. But we do know that once the discovery was made it spread rapidly. There were farmers in Egypt 8000 years ago, and not long after that in Mesopotamia. In some places, archaeologists have actually found ancient stores of grain. In others, they assume that grain was grown because they have found stone sickles with their edges worn from cutting grain.

The ancient farmers of the Middle East cultivated several kinds of wheat, barley and millet. Later, the knowledge of farming spread to more and more people.

It was millet that was most important in Africa. Many of the African people never knew wheat, and they didn't know the arts of baking that went along with it. Their staple food was a porridge of millet flour, such as the Bachiga still eat.

It was wheat farming, however, which spread into Europe; but it took a long time to reach there. Our North European ancestors roamed the forests for thousands of years as hunters while complicated civilizations were growing up in Egypt and Babylon.

egyptian forked stick plow

medieval reaper

roman plow

modern tractor drawn plow

hand scythe

What about the American Indian farmers? The Indians came to America from Asia long before farming — probably about 25,000 years ago. Slowly they spread over the whole hemisphere, from the arctic North to the southern tip in Tierra del Fuego.

For thousands of years these people were more or less cut off from the rest of the world. There were, no doubt, occasional contacts. It seems possible that in early times travelers sometimes crossed the Pacific to or from the islands in the South Sea. Later, we know Leif Ericson and other Scandinavians reached the North Atlantic shores, because we have found remains of several little colonies.

But scientists are sure that the knowledge of farming developed independently, among the Indians, and did not come from these visitors.

One reason they think so is that both the foods and the farming methods were different in America. Corn, tomatoes, potatoes, beans of many kinds, squash, chili peppers and many other vegetables first grew only in the New World. Tobacco, too, came originally from the American Indians. We think of Ireland as the home of the potato, and so it is, but only an adopted home. And Indian corn has become so much at home in Africa that the Africans have important legends about how their ancestors discovered it and learned to plant it.

88

The chief Old World foods were not known to the Indians, either. Wheat, barley, millet, rye, cabbages, apples are only a few of the foods that came to America with the European settlers.

The Indians planted their fields in their own ways, too. Most often they used digging sticks rather than the Old World kind of hoe. They softened the ground and hilled it up in little mounds. In each hill a fish was buried. (This was a very good fertilizer.) Then at the top and around the sides of the mound were planted grains of corn, a few beans and some squash seeds.

In the old world, farmers dug up the earth, raked it smooth and then sowed the wheat broadcast. That is, they tossed it out in handfuls as evenly as possible over the field. The seeds were not dug in. That is the way millet is sowed in Africa, too. It is quite different from the procedure familiar to the American Indian farmer.

The only important other cereal in the world was rice. Rice is the chief food of the Far East. It is used in southern China, down into India, and through the islands of the East Indies. It is obvious that all these people learned to use it from each other. Most investigators believe that the people who first planted rice already knew how to grow wheat. Rye came later, and the farmers who developed it certainly knew how to grow other grains.

There were other special discoveries of food plants in the tropics. These were wild foods that needed little cultivation, and could not be transplanted to many different kinds of places. They have never played such an important part in human progress as the cereals did. Although a few of them have become part of the world's diet today — for instance, bananas and pineapples — there are many which you have certainly never tasted, and perhaps never even heard of, like the breadfruit or taro of the South Pacific.

LEARNING TO FARM

During the whole of human history, men developed the art of growing grain for food only two or three times. Most of the people of the world, ancient or modern, who know how to farm, owe this knowledge to the people of just two or three parts of the world, who first developed the technique and subsequently made it available for all mankind.

It seems an awfully simple thing to drop seeds in the earth and watch them grow. How is it that such an important skill as farming was so slow to be perfected, when it seems so simple? Why was it not invented over and over again by many people of the world?

90

It is easy to see why the totem-pole Indians would not have invented it, or the Eskimos. The totem-pole Indians were pretty well off without it, and the Eskimos lived where farming was almost impossible.

But how about other peoples? How about our own ancestors in northern Europe? Why did they wait till they learned it from other people?

The answer can only be that it wasn't so simple and easy as it seems to us. Like other basic inventions, it seems obvious and simple to us because we are so familiar with it that we take it for granted. But it isn't really easy to invent something that involves a very new kind of idea. And farming is more than a new idea, compared with gathering the fruits that nature offers. It also involves a wholly new way of life.

It's easy enough to picture the first step. Science and the writings of imaginative authors are in agreement here. Farming, they tell us, was probably first invented by women, who had to stay closer to whatever home or camp they had in order to take care of the babies and children. In the beginning women probably just cared for wild patches of grain, pulling out weeds and loosening the soil. Then, much later, came the big step of actual planting.

But that step was a long, slow difficult one. Even today there are people who tend wild grain without becoming farmers. The Indians around the Great Lakes make good use of the wild rice that grows there. They take care of the patches and come back year after year to the same place for the harvest. They know about farming from some of their neighbors. But they haven't adopted it for themselves; for a very good reason: they have other sources of food — hunting and fishing — which supply their needs. And they are used to the hunter's way of life. If they were to try to domesticate the wild rice, they would have to change all their habits. Instead of moving on after the harvest to their hunting grounds, they would have to stay and look after the fields.

Women gathering wild rice

So you see, there were lots of different things involved in the invention of farming. It wasn't just a matter of someone's having a bright idea. That may have happened many times. But the group also had to see the point and consider it useful. They had to be willing to take a chance on changing their habits and way of life. The first farmers must have been people with habits that could fit in easily with this new development. And probably something happened to make some change necessary — perhaps the food supply ran out or perhaps there was an increasing number of mouths to feed, so that new ways had to be tried out if they were to go on living where they were. Man usually needs some such goal to jog him out of a familiar rut.

TAMING THE ANIMALS

About the same time that some men were learning to farm, they — or others — were learning to take care of goats and sheep and cows, so that they would be readily available for food. Later on the tended animals also yielded milk and wool for clothing.

Some say the first step toward domesticating animals was taken by men who were already farmers. They suggest that it came about rather simply, through the wild animals' coming to feed on the stubble of cut grain patches. Others point out that the life of the shepherd is different from that of the farmer, and suggest that herding may have been worked out first by other groups of people. We shall have to wait for the archaeologist to uncover more data to solve this riddle, as he goes on with his digging in Asia. Asia was the cradle of almost all man's food animals — cows and goats; sheep; later horses, and probably donkeys as well.

In any case, it seems that herding, like farming, was far harder to invent than we should think. It, too, spread to all parts of the Old World from one central source; it was not just invented over and over again. Even people who use quite different animals like the camel or the reindeer appear to have learned the art from neighbors, and just applied it to animals that were available locally. Chickens are about the only Old World animal that may have trickled in from a separate stream.

Although most of the herding people of the world have learned the art from one source, they learned it at different stages, and some of them use it in very different ways. There are some herdsmen who don't practice the art of milking, and in India they never use their cattle for food. In Africa they have no idea of how to make cheese, and they wouldn't dream of using their cows for riding, or to pull loads.

Whether or not herding began among farmers, it certainly was not always connected with farming. Some

herding people in Asia and Africa live a nomadic life that doesn't go with farming at all. If you follow your flocks and herds to places where grass is available in different seasons, you just aren't around to tend any crop or harvest it. You can't imagine a modern cowboy or gaucho hoeing potatoes, can you? No more could the Mongol herders of Central Asia stoop to such prosaic tasks!

There are neighbors of the Bachiga today who live mostly by herding. They live on sour milk, cooked blood, and meat. They wouldn't dream of farming, or even of eating farm produce. The only exception they make is beer, which is brewed out of millet. But they don't prepare that themselves.

The nomads of the Asiatic plains use their herds for everything too; the animals on which they depend are horses. They ride them and milk them and eat their flesh, and they use their hides in many ways. These people are not ignorant of farming — they disdain it.

In no place in the New World except Peru were any animals domesticated — except, of course, the dog, which seems to have attached himself to man quite early in his wanderings.

In Peru, the llama and the alpaca were tamed; their wool was used, and they sometimes carried burdens. But the use of these animals never spread beyond the slopes of the Andes. Some Indians did keep a few half-wild turkeys for food, but this was not a central point in their way of life.

The Eskimos, cut off from the streams of herding knowledge, never tamed the caribou. We know now that it can be tamed; it is quite like the Asiatic reindeer. At one point, our government imported great herds of tame reindeer from Siberia to graze in our own arctic, and they got on perfectly well.

You will perhaps wonder why people so resourceful as the Eskimos did not make this discovery and raise caribou, as they made so many other discoveries — even if they could not learn about it from their neighbors. One reason is this: The caribou was not as important in the lives of most Eskimos, as were seals and walrus. Spring and summer were not the central time in their lives, nor even, according to the explorer Stefansson, the pleasantest. When the thaw began, they moved inland and hunted the caribou. But they thought of the warm days as a rather disagreeable time that had to be endured until the ice froze and they could hunt seal again. Stefansson tells how he looked forward to spring during his first winter in the arctic. But when it came it was terrible! The snow houses began to melt, and everyone moved into tents, which were very leaky. And there were swarms of mosquitoes. He himself was very glad when he had the good, secure feeling of ice and snow around him again.

In any case, it seems that once the early ancestors of the Eskimos began to get used to the North, all their inventive ideas were centered on their winter living. Their religion helped to keep the distinction clear. You remember that they were not allowed to use deer knives or any other summer things in the wintertime, lest they endanger the seal hunting. There wouldn't be much point in herding reindeer if they could be used only a few months in the year! Herding would certainly not be just a simple addition to Eskimo living. It would require a complete change in all their life ways. This is not the kind of situation in which invention grows. Such difficulties even stand in the way of people's borrowing inventions from their neighbors, let alone working them out for themselves.

FARMING PROVIDES NEW OPPORTUNITIES

Archaeologists have a name for the period we have been talking about, when men first learned to farm and to keep animals. They call it the NEOLITHIC, which means the New Stone Age. Actually the name isn't a very good one. It comes from a new tool, great polished stone axes that some farming people used to clear the forests, so that grain could be planted. But the important thing is not the stone tools. It is the fact that men had learned to farm.

Even in its simplest forms, farming life brings important changes to people and to their ways of living together. You see, when men hunt and fish, dig up wild roots and collect seeds to get their living, they never know from one day to the next what their luck will be like. Even their most reliable supplies are limited, and they have no way of increasing them.

But when men learn to grow their own food, they can increase the supply. Because of this, the population can increase. The same area which supported only a few hunters can safely support hundreds of people who grow grain on it. My Bachiga friends, for example, are not particularly efficient farmers. Their fields are none too fertile, their farming methods crude. But even inefficient Bachiga methods produce enough food for a large population. The whole of their country is only a few days' walk in any direction, yet there are tens of thousands of Bachiga people. In this tiny territory there are more Bachiga than there are Eskimos over the whole northland from Alaska to Greenland.

Farmers live in more settled villages than most hunters. Even the poorest of them must stay in one place for a few years at a time, if they are to work their fields and be there to gather the crops. They can put more time, effort and materials into their houses, and they can store clothing and utensils for future use. Because more food is available, people can afford to take time to practice other skills, relying on exchange with their neighbors to eke out their food supply. A specialized worker can make far more improvements than a Jack-of-all-trades, for he has more knowledge and experience of the particular materials to be dealt with. Crafts like pottery are widely associated with farming life, and it was in farming communities that complicated skills like weaving and metalworking were finally developed.

These are new opportunities for living and working together. They also raise all sorts of new problems.

Even the simplest, poorest farmers need rules about the land. How is it to be assigned to different people? And how divide the harvest? Shall each family work its own plot and enjoy the fruits of its own labor? Quarrels may arise about boundaries or trespassing or the water supply. Some sorts of rules are necessary to take care of all such difficulties, and there have to be ways of enforcing them. If there are special craftsmen, they need some agreement upon ways of exchanging their goods. After all, markets aren't a usual part of living among simple hunting people. And because farmers could accumulate more goods, and would have full granaries after the harvest, they were in danger of raids and attacks. They had to have ways of protecting themselves.

As they faced these new problems, farming people developed new ways of living together. Some of these were similar in different parts of the world, because the problems were similar. But there were vast differences, too. Each farming group had its own particular problems. Some lived where land was rich and fertile, others struggled with poor soil and drought. Some had to hunt as well as farm; others kept sheep or pigs.

There was another reason, too, why farming people developed different cultures. Remember, no group had learned to farm before about 10,000 years ago. When people did learn, they already had long years of history behind them. They had already worked out many different ways of living and working together. So when they began to farm, they didn't just drop all their old ways and start over again from scratch. They didn't sit down and say, "What would be the ideal way to live under these new conditions?" Instead, they muddled along — building their new ways on their old customs and traditions, and retaining as much of their differing old ways of life as could possibly be fitted in.

Let's have a look, now, at some of the primitive farming people of the modern world, and see how people lived who knew how to farm, but had not built cities or machines to work for them, who had not learned to write and who were not yet part of the complex interrelated life that we call civilization.

9.

THE BACHIGA PEOPLE

WE left my Bachiga friends digging their fields with simple iron hoes, and tending their flocks and herds. You remember that although the Bachiga have these advantages over some of the other primitive farmers, their technical skills are still very simple. Even today they have no plows or machinery of any sort. They don't put any of their animals to work. And they don't know about using fertilizers to increase their crops.

Their ways of living together are quite simple too. They live in small villages. All the people who live in each village are related to each other. Families are nearly self-supporting, and villages completely so. There is no united Bachiga tribe, no tribal chiefs or government. People are just Bachiga because they speak the same language and live the same way.

The Bachiga know many more kinds of people than the Eskimos do, yet their world is far smaller than ours.

FARMERS AND CRAFTSMEN

The way in which a Bachiga farmer gets his living is very different from that of a farmer in our country. Our own farmers are workers who specialize in growing food or other products — but not just for their own use. They sell their produce for money, which they use to buy other things they need. Many dairy farmers buy all their butter at the grocery store in town. And the wives of wheat farmers often use bakery bread, or if they bake their own, buy the flour for making it.

Bachiga farmers don't think in terms of markets or prices. They are content to produce the food that their own families will eat — and if possible, to grow enough so that they can brew plenty of beer. Every family makes its own clothing and some of its own tools. When a man wants to build a house he prepares all the materials himself — posts and papyrus ropes and grass bundles for thatching the roof. Then he gets all his neighbors to help him put it up. They like to do the actual building all in one day. There is a big feast, and lots of merriment for everyone who comes to help.

103

Putting up the sides

Frame is thatched over...

Bachiga families aren't as completely independent as Eskimo families are. They need their neighbors for this kind of task. They need them to protect themselves against danger of raids or marauding animals. And they also need the occasional services of a skilled craftsman. Not everyone could possibly be a blacksmith. It takes too many years of learning, too much equipment. It doesn't make sense for everyone in the village to own all the different kinds of axes and adzes that an expert carpenter needs, either. Sometimes it is convenient to get someone more skilled to help make pots or tan hides, and everyone needs to consult different kinds of herb doctors as well as diviners and priests from time to time.

If you are a Bachiga, these specialized skills are all available in your own or the next-door village. But you can't just go out and buy the products. If as a Bachiga you want a hoe, you have to go to a blacksmith and arrange to have him make you one. Perhaps you will supply him with scrap iron from old tools, to reforge into something new. You will probably hang around while he works, and you may help a little by fetching water or pumping the bellows. But you will also have to pay him. The approximate amount is fixed by custom, but you will dicker for a while about the precise terms.

For less important specialists, the arrangements are less formal. One of my friends was an expert pot maker. When she was ready to make a batch of pots, her neighbors would beg her to make a pot or two for them. There would be no actual payment, but they would take whatever opportunity they could to make a return gift. And they would help a little with the work — carrying clay from the clay pits which are some distance away from the village, and gathering the special grasses for the very hot fires needed for the ovens.

There are quite a number of specializing craftsmen in a village, if you count everyone who knows a little of a particular kind of magic, or some kind of curing, or how to carve stools, and so on. But none of them ever make a full-time job of practicing their crafts. That isn't the way they make their living. All of them live like everyone else on food raised by their own families in their own gardens.

A Bachiga considers anyone very unfortunate who has to buy grain, or meat, or hides. He would not want to give up his independence even for what seems to us far greater wealth. A few people have broken with this tradition. They live on wages made by working in the small European settlement nearby. But most people are sorry for them. Everyone wept when a girl in our village married one of these townsmen, though he was quite well off. They thought it was dreadful that she would have to buy her food in the market place.

Most people who work for Europeans prefer to keep their own homes and farms in the old way. Only by doing this are they self-supporting in their own eyes.

Because every family owns its means of getting a living and needs only a few things it cannot make for itself, Bachiga ideas about work and profit are quite different from ours — though they would seem very sensible and obvious to many of the peoples of the world. No one has to work for anyone else, unless it suits him. Such a situation has often caused misunderstandings. Perhaps you have heard it said that primitive people are lazy, because they do not choose to work long and hard for pay. But the questions that have to be asked are: Why should they? What have they to gain by it?

Our means of production are expensive and are owned by a limited number of people. So we *have* to work for a living, usually for someone else, and sometimes on whatever terms we can get. We have accepted this, and our ideas of work and profit fit in with it. But attitudes are quite different among people who do everything more simply and independently, and who produce chiefly for their own families. In such a group there is no pressure on a craftsman to work more than he wants to work.

This difference in attitudes can often lead to situations surprising to anyone but an anthropologist. An American tourist once visited a Mexican craftsman who had a beautiful hand-painted chair for sale. The maker quoted a price for it, and the American said he would like to order a dozen just like it. "In that case," said the craftsman, "they will cost you more. I don't like to make so many all exactly alike." Although the Mexicans' way of life is far less simple than the Bachiga's, some of their attitudes are similar. They are not easily understood by Americans who have accepted our system in which things get cheaper when they are produced in larger quantities.

WOMEN WORK HARD

The heaviest work on American farms is done by men. Occasionally women drive tractors or ride hay rakes, and many women work along with men, hoeing and picking crops by hand. But farming in general is considered man's work in which women share.

Among the Bachiga people, work in the fields is the job of the women, not of the men. It is the women who prepare the earth and plant the seeds, hoe and harvest the crops. They even bring most of the harvest home from the fields, carrying great basketloads down from the hills on their heads.

Bachiga women work very hard indeed. They have the whole responsibility of making sure that there will be enough food grown and stored from one harvest to the next. Mothers really need their daughters' help, and in families where the mother is lazy, or if she happens to be ill, it is sometimes difficult to make ends meet. Most of the Bachiga women I knew felt that they had no time to relax but must be always working. At one wedding party I attended, many of the guests spent the second morning sleeping after a long night of dancing and feasting. But a number of the girls, who had stayed up just as late as

the others, got up early in the morning and rushed off to put in a few hours' work in the fields before the dancing started again.

Perhaps you may wonder what Bachiga men do with their time. They cut down the bushes where new land has to be cleared for farming or building. They build the houses and keep them repaired. They see that all the tools are ready for use. They have charge of the cows. (Actually, they manage to leave most of the routine herding, except for the milking, to the growing boys.) The men used to hunt a good deal, but now the British Government has declared a general closed season for reasons of conservation. Some of them practice the special crafts we've spoken of. And they do have some leisure time to gossip and smoke, to visit and drink beer and engage in endless discussions about a trade or a marriage.

THE LAND

Owning land is very important to an American farmer. A man will work very hard to earn enough to buy his own farm, or enlarge it. And there are lots of tenant farmers and sharecroppers who cannot enjoy the full harvest that they grow because someone else owns the land and they must pay for its use.

Bachiga conditions are more like ours were in pioneer days. There isn't any shortage of land. There is still land out in the wilderness which is unclaimed. A man can stake a claim to it if he is willing to work it. Close to the village, it is important to know which portion belongs to which man, and to respect each other's rights, even when land is not being planted by its owner at the moment.

But there is one important difference from our pioneer land conditions. If a Bachiga's whole neighborhood has grown crowded, and he wants to move farther away, he can't always do it. For every neighborhood is settled by kinsmen, people who are at least distantly related to each other. He can't move into other people's empty bush land. And there is no way of buying his way into the situation. He just has to gather his friends, drive out the people settled there, and turn it into his own family's territory.

Even within the village there are sometimes arguments. Kasagara may claim that Bitanachi has planted peas in land that really belongs to Kasagara, land that Kasagara was simply allowing to lie fallow for a while. Or Njuyargo may claim that someone's cows have been allowed to stray in his grainfield. This kind of dispute is all in the family, and is settled by a kind of arbitration proceeding that the Bachiga love. It amounts to a kind of hearing before a court. Both sides present their arguments with passion and vigor, and summon all the witnesses they can. There isn't any regular judge; any respected member of the community can sit in judgment, and almost everybody else will stand around and give an opinion, too.

Quarrels outside the family are far more serious, whether they're about land or about cattle-raiding or about anything else, because there isn't anybody to arbitrate between families. If you are a Bachiga you can't do anything about it but fight it out. You count on the support of your own group of relatives to help you in such a fight — not just the close relatives who live in your own villages, but more distant ones as well, who live in neighboring villages but who also count as your brothers and sisters.

We call such a large group of relatives a "clan," after the Scottish families which acted in a somewhat similar way, protecting each other and taking vengeance on outsiders. Clans of this sort are very common among primitive farming people of the world, though the exact way they work out varies a little. Certainly, they don't all engage in the fierce feuds that the Bachiga clans do. These sometimes become so exaggerated, that it isn't safe to travel at all outside your own clan's lands, and the proudest boast anyone can have is that he killed a member of an enemy clan.

The Bachiga people make a clear distinction between murder and killing. It is murder when you put to death someone in your own group, and you must be punished for it. It is a justifiable killing when you put to death someone in another group who is the enemy of your group. This distinction runs through all of human history. And we still make it. We justify fighting in wars, while we have laws against any other sort of killing. Some people even claim that war is a "natural" and inevitable way of settling disputes, though scientists know that there is no evidence to support such an idea. In fact, there is evidence that people can extend the old idea of kinship. The group which is regarded as that of fellow men, whose killing is always murder, has been growing larger: from clan to community to nation, till now it is beginning to reach out tentatively to include the whole world.

The Bachiga have a very simple idea of group responsibility, and it has led to permanent feuds between clans. Other people have managed the problem differently. They have often organized several clans into a larger group that can work together peacefully. Since the Bachiga don't have such an organization, they have worked out an ingenious way of making deals between clans. For example, they have a rule that you *must* marry someone who is outside your own clan, because members of your own clan are considered your brothers and sisters. But how can a man arrange for a wife if he is likely to be killed

113

the minute he sets foot in another clan's territory?

To solve this problem, they have a "blood-brotherhood pact." This is how it works: Two men from different clans meet and sit down opposite each other. A tiny cut is made in the arm of each one, and a few grains of millet are rubbed into the blood. Then each swallows the millet dipped in the other's blood. And at the same time they swear a mighty oath:

> *If I should ever spear you, may this blood which I am swallowing swell up in me till I burst! If I should ever fail to come to your aid in distress, may the blood which I am swallowing swell up in me till I burst! If I should betray your trust or steal from you, may this blood swell up in me till I burst!*

The Bachiga hold this oath very sacred. From then on, the men who have taken it are above any clan feuding. They would sooner cheat their own brother than a blood-pact brother. And so it is through the pact-brothers that all business between clans is done.

The British have put an end to a good deal of the fighting between Bachiga clans, and it is not so important to have a series of pact-brothers as it used to be. But people do still "swallow blood together," and they help each other as much as possible.

The Bachiga household, the family of fathers and mothers and children who live together, is quite different from ours.

How would you like to live in your grandfather's house, with innumerable cousins, ten grandmothers, and three mothers? It isn't quite like that for all Bachiga children, but it is for some.

You see, a Bachiga man may marry several wives, just as many as he can afford. Lots of men do marry anywhere from two or three to ten and even more. Each wife has a house of her own, but they are all in one compound. And when a man's sons grow up and marry, they bring their wives home to father's compound, and settle down there too. They haven't any choice in the matter, either. Papa is boss, and that's that. As long as he's alive, his sons are all junior. They do as he says. He owns the fields, he assigns them sections for their wives to work, he makes all kinds of decisions for them; he even decides whom they are to marry.

It isn't just that they need his permission to marry — he does all the actual choosing, and makes all the arrangements.

To us this seems an outrageous idea. People are different, and we don't always like the same people our parents do, though they may be very worthy characters. Perhaps you've heard the expression, "After all, I don't intend to marry her family." In the Bachiga way of arranging things, the whole family *is* involved. The bride comes to live in her father-in-law's household; she really becomes a member of that family group. Of course, they are all concerned in the choice.

Besides, there really aren't as many kinds of differences between Bachiga people as are possible in our way of life. Everyone has been brought up in much the same way, and has about the same ideas and standards.

So, when any two people marry, they are bound to have a great deal in common. One husband may be a little older or a little younger than another, a little lazier or a little more hard-working. One may play the flute and another may get into fights when he is drunk. But these things are only a small part of daily living. There is no danger that a wife who likes night clubs will find herself married to a man who can't even dance, or that a girl with ambitions for a career will have a husband who thinks woman's place is in the kitchen. Such widely different possibilities don't even exist among the Bachiga. There are kind people and selfish ones, gentle ones and quick-tempered. But for the most part all the Bachiga spend their time in much the same way, and see eye-to-eye about all really important things, because for them there just isn't any other way at all to see.

These arranged marriages, therefore, are not nearly so hard for Bachiga young people to take as they would be for us. What is more, that is the only respectable way they know for a marriage to take place. Everyone in their world was married that way. Many of them are quite happy, living together in peace and harmony, sharing responsibilities and the care of their children. Of course, not all their marriages are happy. But neither are all of ours, even though ours are based on the personal choice of the bride and groom.

After all, even for us marriage is not a strictly private and personal matter; it means children, and the way children are cared for concerns the whole group — not just the parents. Even in our society, the community plays some part in marriage. Everyone has to take out a marriage license. If the bride is too young according to our customs, she needs her parents' consent. Although children are chiefly their parents' responsibility, the community does take care of their schooling, and it gives them some health supervision. If parents really neglect a child, it may even order him taken away from them.

We take care of all these things through school boards, courts, health officers. People like the Bachiga have no such machinery for solving problems; they work things out through the family, in which a married couple is only one part of a much larger group. And so it is natural that the larger family group should have some say about marriage itself.

PAPA FOOTS THE BILL

The Bachiga father has to do more than just choose the husband or wife for his child. He has to foot the bill.

It isn't the bride's father that pays. It's the groom's father.

It isn't the wedding cost that counts so much, either, though that may mount up — what with sheep for feasting, and lots of beer. The principal cost is what is usually called the bride-price, though really we don't have a word for it, because we haven't any such practice.

In the Bachiga world, when a man marries he must pay the bride's father a kind of marriage portion or dowry, in cattle. The exact amount is arranged in advance, in a long series of discussions. The more important the two families, the larger the amount.

The Bachiga don't look on this as buying a wife. That is no more involved than in our custom of presenting a girl with a diamond ring on becoming engaged. The bride's father isn't even supposed to put the cattle he receives into his regular herd. He is supposed to keep them as a unit, and use them to arrange another marriage, particularly one for the girl's brother.

Of course, a man with large herds can afford to marry many wives, and a poor man will have few. A poor man's sons may have to wait until their sisters marry before they can hope to get a bride.

THE WEDDING

A Bachiga wedding is a grand occasion that lasts for several days. But the strangest part of it is that the groom isn't on hand for the first part of it at all. And as for the bride, she is supposed to spend all her time at it crying!

As we have seen, the bride and groom must always come from different clans, from different villages. The girl is told nothing of the plans that are being made until the actual day of the wedding arrives. She doesn't know who her groom is and probably has never seen him before.

When the groom's relatives arrive at her home, she rushes off to hide. While the wedding guests feast and dance, she sits in the back room of the house with her parents and weeps. In the end, her brothers have to come and drag her out by force. At this point a good show is expected. All her girl friends rush to help her, and they are pulled out one by one, fighting and shrieking. Finally, the bride's brothers seize her and carry her off to the groom's home, accompanied by his relatives.

120

The groom himself has not yet appeared at the ceremonies at all. He is waiting at the gate of his father's compound to receive the bride. She is expected to keep up a steady sobbing protest all the way to her new home, and for at least a day afterward, while the groom's friends have a merry feast with her brothers.

There is a good reason for the bride's tears and misery — but it is not the reason that might come to your mind first. She does not suffer because she has missed a romantic marriage — she wouldn't even understand such an idea. But she does feel keenly the separation from her own family and the fact that from now on she must belong to another family, all of whom are strangers to her.

Wedding dance

GROWING UP

Since the Bachiga people have no romantic ideas about courtship and marriage, life for their teen-agers is very different from ours. They have no dates, no chance for flirtation or falling in love. Young people do go to parties, but they are heavily chaperoned, and boys and girls do not dance together. The girls form a chorus to beat out a rhythm for the men's dancing. Anyway, most of the young men at parties are their own brothers and cousins, and the few visitors who do come are so busy with formalities that they have no time for flirting. No well-brought-up Bachiga girl would ever talk familiarly with a stranger. She would not talk with him at all, except in the presence of a chaperone. She must be shy and retiring, and wait for her father to choose a husband for her. A girl who giggled and showed any interest in a boy would be considered very bad and immodest.

They marry much younger than we do. There is no reason why they shouldn't. No one has to wait till he has finished his education. If there were an unmarried girl of sixteen she would be an old maid, but that just doesn't happen, although a young man may have to postpone his wedding for a while if his family is poor.

CATTLE ARE WEALTH

You remember that among the Eskimos and the Australians there were no differences in wealth, but among
the fishermen of the Pacific Coast, who had more material goods, there were chiefs far wealthier than other
people. They had social position and power.

Most farming people had far more material goods than
the Eskimos or the Australians. They could make more
kinds of things, out of more materials. They could keep
them longer.

But not all of them placed great value on being rich.
Later on you are going to read something about some of
our American Indian farming people, who just didn't
have the idea of individuals' getting rich at all.

Among the Bachiga, differences in wealth did exist.
But they only made a small difference in the way people
lived, and being wealthy didn't mean having very much
power or any special social position. The only kind of
wealth they count is wealth in cattle. Land-owning doesn't
mean wealth. Everyone can go out and use all the land
he needs. The Bachiga never developed ways that would
allow one man to own a lot of property and make other
people work on it for him. The ownership of tools or

ornaments doesn't mean wealth. There is very little difference in these things between one family and another. But having lots of cows is important.

Cattle are important not only for their own direct use or to produce food. Butter is useful, especially as an ointment, but one or two cows could supply a family's need for butter quite adequately. Sour milk isn't an important part of their diet, as it is for some of their herding neighbors, and not even a very wealthy man would think of killing a cow just for its meat or hides, though he would use both if the animal died.

The real value of cows isn't any of this. It's their use as bride-price!

A man with lots of cattle can marry many wives. And since Bachiga women do the main work in the fields, more wives mean more crops. Of course, one or two hardworking wives can raise enough food for the family to eat. But more wives means there will be plenty of grain for beer, and workers to brew it. A man with many wives can do a lot of entertaining, and maintain an important place in village life.

Sometimes a man with cows can use them to get other people to work for him. A very poor man with no cows — and no way, therefore, of getting a wife — will be ready to come and beg a richer man for a cow so he can get

married. Afterwards he will have to come to his bene-
factor often with gifts of grain and beer, and dance in his
praise at feasts.

But there aren't many Bachiga who are either that
wealthy or that poor, as is the case among some of their
neighbors, where there are wealthy overlords who monop-
olize all the cattle, and keep a court of dependent young
men to herd for them and fight for them.

ANCESTORS AND DIVINERS

What is the Bachiga religion like?

Well, it's a little surprising in some ways. We might
expect a farming people to center their religion around
their need for fertile land and good harvests. That is the
main thing in many of the ancient religions that we know
about. And so it is among many primitive farming people
of the world today.

But that isn't the main thing in Bachiga religion.

The Bachiga people don't think they need the help of
their gods to make their crops grow. They rather take it
for granted that seeds, given normal weather conditions,
will yield a normal harvest. They think of the world as
more or less going on its own course smoothly enough,
except when something bad happens to disturb it. But of

125

course, bad things do sometimes happen. A swarm of locusts or a sudden hailstorm may destroy an entire harvest in one day. Obviously, there must be evil forces in the universe that make such things happen, and that cause people to fall ill and die. *These* forces are worth worrying about. Good gods will be good, without man's having to do too much about it. But evil spirits need to be treated kindly, given gifts of beer and even sheep or cows, so that they will not cause trouble.

Many of the peoples of the world practice ancestor worship. Usually it is a source of pride to them, and they feel secure in having a whole line of ancestors on their side. But if you are a Bachiga it is different. Your own ancestors are just another nuisance — one more possible cause of illness and other troubles. You build a ghost hut in your compound, where you can make sacrifices to your many different ancestral spirits. But you don't do it indiscriminately. You are too practical for that. You don't bother to sacrifice to those ghosts who haven't proved that they intend to cause trouble. You give offerings instead to those who have somehow made their malice and their power clear.

To find out what particular ghost is causing illness or any other bad luck, or whether such misfortune is due to some other kind of spirit, or perhaps to witchcraft

practiced by some human enemy, you go to a diviner.

A diviner is a kind of fortuneteller. He is supposed to be able to read the truth about the spirits in many ways — by examining blobs of suds in a bowl of water, by studying the markings in the entrails of a fresh-killed baby chicken, or by tossing up marked sticks and seeing how they fall.

This kind of belief is very common all over the world. Even today, in our most modern cities, people go to fortunetellers who read their palms or cast horoscopes or consult cards or tea leaves. They go to "mediums" who stare into crystal globes or claim to make strange voices talk, and see luminous figures floating in the air.

In our society, people are usually worried about the future, because they feel so insecure. They ask: "Will I be rich?" or "Am I going to get married?"

The Bachiga are more concerned about the past. They want to find out what has already happened so that they can control the future. They want to know what they did wrong. When they find that out, they believe they can set things right, and get rid of trouble — for a while at least.

The diviner whom they consult may tell them to make a sacrifice to a deceased uncle, or to take a live sheep to a man who claims to have special dealings with a spirit snake that lives in the rocks. Or he may discover that someone has broken some important rule which automatically makes for trouble. Perhaps a careless girl sat on a grindstone? That will surely bring disaster. If one ate out of a bowl that his dead grandmother once ate out of, he is sure to get leprosy! The spirits don't *bring* these punishments: they are immediate dangers, as automatic as infection from drinking polluted water. Just as we call a doctor, the Bachiga call a diviner to find the cause and suggest a cure.

It's hard for us to understand a religion that is so concerned with evil things, or to see how people can picture their gods as so mean.

But this really fits right in with Bachiga ideas of human nature. They don't like and trust each other very much. Brothers help each other because they have to, for their own safety, but they often suspect each other of secret plots. Of course, the Bachiga don't admire people who are quarrelsome and treacherous. They avoid associating with them as much as possible. But they don't actually do anything about getting rid of them. There was one man in Bufuka who was suspected of being both a thief and a sorcerer. Nobody liked to visit at his house or work with him; but they invited him to weddings and other affairs, because he was a relative and they had to.

So you see Bachiga religion parallels in many ways their daily lives and their relations with each other. Life itself is insecure and no man can trust anyone outside his own clan. Neither can he trust the spirits. And the Bachiga have no regular government with chiefs and laws for everybody, so we can't expect to find formal priests, or tribal gods that everybody worships. Each family and clan is concerned only with its own spirits, or a few miscel-

laneous racketeering ones that belong to no one in particular. None of the spirits are concerned with good behavior, or making man's lot good. They are, rather, a kind
of symbol of all the hardships and difficulties that men
face.

NO COMPETITION!

Such is Bachiga life. To my Bachiga friend Eseri and
her family, everything about it seemed obvious and natural. They couldn't imagine any other way of living or
thinking. After I had told them about my own country,
they found many things hard to believe, and they quizzed
me over and over again.

How could girls get married without a proper bride-
price? Was it really true that girls could fall in love, *want*
to get married, and choose their own husbands? And
everyone approved? This idea was too shocking to believe — although it was not exactly unattractive.

They could not see, either, why we should want to kill
cattle just to eat them. And as for putting precious cattle
to work in any way — that was just barbaric.

Even harder to understand was our habit of "keeping
up with the Joneses." Why should anyone care whether
his clothes or his belongings were more elegant than any-

one else's? Eseri rather liked to decorate the baskets she made — but that was just a personal whim, a matter of taste. It wouldn't get her a better husband. It wouldn't even win her praise from other people. After all, my Bachiga friends liked to point out, "You can drink just as well from a plain cup as from a decorated one."

In our society business works by competing. We reflect this in all our ideas about success, including marks in school, and even dating! Mary is unhappy if Jane has twice as many dates. But among the Bachiga there is no background for this kind of competition. Bachiga men admire a good big household, with lots of wives and lots of cattle. But there isn't any way of getting these at the expense of your neighbor; in fact, there aren't even any very direct ways of working for them. For the ordinary man, it's largely a matter of luck — a good proportion of daughters, and cattle that multiply well. Otherwise only a man with a powerful spirit, or a warrior leader, whom we might call a brigand, could amass cattle. Even the richest Bachiga can never have a very large herd, because their pasture lands are not good enough to feed many cattle.

There is plenty of room in such a setup for envy and jealousy, traits of which the Bachiga are very well aware; but none for competition or ambition, which seem so obvious to us.

10.

INDIAN FARMERS

THE Bachiga are African farmers. They have cows and metal hoes, which are not available to the many farming people of other parts of the world. Some of their social customs are also usual African ones. Many other African tribes also pay a bride-price for their wives, consider cattle very important as wealth, and give enormous authority to the father.

Such traditions are not found in quite the same way among other farming peoples, though many of them do have clans and believe in the spirits of their ancestors.

Let's have a look at one of the American Indian farming peoples, a Southwestern group like the Zuni or the Hopi. These Indians have insisted upon maintaining their own ways. Up to a few years ago, they would not even let traders or tourists into their villages. So we can still talk

132

about them and study them as they were before schools and money and harvesting machines began to change the picture somewhat.

We shall pretend we are visiting one of their villages as it was about forty years ago.

These Southwestern Indians live in large communities which the Spaniards called pueblos. Such a village looks like one huge apartment house, several stories high. Over two thousand people live in it, and it is a fortress as well as a house. There are no outside doors on the first floors at all. To get inside, everybody must climb up log ladders to a terrace, then through holes in the roof and down other ladders to windowless apartments. This is inconvenient, but it makes the village safe from enemies. The ladders can just be pulled up when other tribes try to get in and steal the stored corn, or the fine blankets and beautiful ornaments which the Pueblo Indians make so well.

Actually the lack of windows and doors is no great hardship. For most of the important things are done outside on the high terraces in the dry desert air. Here pots are shaped and blankets woven. Here the women carry on the almost endless daily task of grinding corn between stones. Singing, they roll their stone tools in rhythm to make beautiful colored meal from the yellow or blue or white grains. Much of the baking is done in outdoor

ovens, too, although paper-thin bread and vegetables are cooked on hot stones over indoor fireplaces.

Corn and squash and beans — these are the main foods in the pueblo, with rabbit and small game only seldom to be had, for animals have a hard time living in almost desert country. So little rain falls that vegetable gardens must be planted near streams, from which water can be carried in jars or routed through irrigation ditches. The gardens are quite close to the pueblo, where the women can care for them. But the huge cornfields often are planted a long way from the village. During the busy part of the season, the field-workers can't make the trip back and forth every day, and so they must camp out, unprotected from their enemies. It is not surprising that it is the men, rather than the women, who take care of these exposed cornfields.

We saw that Bachiga women grow the grain. Among Pueblo Indians, this task is assigned to the men. There are differences like this in the tasks assigned to men and women all over the world. Work is divided in many different ways, and, of course, each people is inclined to think that its own ways are right and proper, peculiarly suited to men's and women's special nature. In our culture, for example, spinning has always been women's work — we even call an unmarried woman a spinster.

135

And we teach girls, not boys, to knit and embroider. But spinning is men's work in many parts of the world. It is Pueblo men who weave the cloth and blankets. A milkmaid is a perfectly natural thing to us, but for a Bachiga man the idea is shocking. To him, care of the cattle is a purely masculine job. There are places in the world where women carry burdens on their heads with greater ease and grace than men, and one such people will tell you, "Everyone knows that women's heads are naturally harder than men's!" (If you think that is silly remember you have probably heard — and maybe you even believe — that women "don't drive automobiles as well as men." But insurance company records show that quite the reverse is true!) Cooking is men's work in Polynesia. Warfare and hunting are about the only tasks that almost all people assign regularly to men, and child-rearing the one they all usually assign to women, though men take over the teaching at various different ages.

So far as anthropologists have discovered, there is no such thing as a "proper" task for a man or a woman — as if everywhere the one had a natural ability to do certain things and the other did not. The division of tasks in all cultures they have found has nothing to do with *ability;* it is based, instead, upon the *needs and habits* of the group.

136

Among the Pueblo Indians, men do the work in the fields, but they don't own them. The women do. The women own the fields and the houses. When a man marries, he goes to live with his wife's family. If they quarrel, it's he who has to go home to mother!

Pueblo men don't have any important say in their wives' households. They aren't really full members of the family; they are more like permanent guests, who earn their keep. A Pueblo father doesn't even have real authority over his children. He makes them toys, teaches them and plays games with them. But it isn't up to him to scold them, or to make important decisions for them. That's the job of other members of the family — uncles. (Mother's brothers — not father's, for whom we use the same word, "uncle." You can be sure that they don't.)

This sounds like the reverse of Bachiga family life, but it isn't really. Among the Bachiga the women have no authority at all. They are junior members of their husband's household, with no say anywhere. Zuni or Hopi men have plenty of authority. The only thing is, they have it in their own homes, not in their wives' homes. A man goes back to his mother's apartment for family ceremonies; he has to make all the important decisions for his sister's children who live there, his nieces and nephews.

Perhaps this sounds mixed-up and complicated? You may wonder how a child keeps it all straight! But it isn't very confusing when you live with it. As a Zuni child, you live at home with your mother and your grandmother. Your father, whom you adore, lives with you, too, but on important ceremonial days, he goes off to his mother's family altar, and your uncles come home to worship. They hold family councils, and if necessary speak to your mother about your behavior, or about your future. For example, they will decide with her whether it is time for you to be initiated into a religious society.

Your uncles have definite authority, but they certainly aren't as bossy as a Bachiga father. People just don't order each other around that way in Pueblo society. Marriage, especially, is something young people can be left to settle for themselves, since it's all in the same village anyway.

PUEBLO CLANS

Since the family that lives together consists of a mother, her married daughters and their children, it won't surprise you to learn that the Pueblo clan is made up the same way, through generation after generation of mothers and daughters, and their daughters and daughters' daughters. In each generation the sons are very important. They perform the religious ceremonies and hold tribal positions representing their clans. But their children won't hold these offices after them. Their children don't belong to the same clan; they belong to their mother's clan.

To us this seems a very strange way of reckoning kinship, and so it would to the Bachiga. But it would be very familiar to lots of other farming people, not only among the Indians, but in the South Pacific too. It is a way so widely known that anthropologists have even given it a name. (It's MATRILINY, for those of you who want to know.)

The fact that kinship and ownership of houses and land are all reckoned through the women seems quite strange to us in Pueblo living because after all the men do the main productive work in the fields. Among other American Indian farming groups, like the Iroquois, such family arrangements seem more natural and fitting, for among the Iroquois the women work in the gardens more or less on their own. The men are away a good deal of the time, hunting and fighting. It is from such traditions that the culture of the Southwest stems, and upon which they have built their somewhat more complicated ways.

The Bachiga village was a small group of close relatives. Neighboring villages were made up of other families belonging to the same clan. The Pueblo village is an entirely different kind of thing. It *is* the entire tribe! It is made up of many different families, grouped into clans, and these clans, instead of being separate and feuding, are co-operative parts of a very close and harmonious community.

Each clan owns land, which it apportions among its members. It has certain apartments, in which its members live, and it appoints representatives to the village council, which settles all community affairs. The clans all work very closely together. They give great dances and feasts, and see to it that families who have had bad luck in planting or harvesting are given harvest gifts, so that all will be provided for. This isn't a task left to close relatives; it is everybody's business. The primary concern in all matters is the well-being and harmony of the entire Pueblo. Perhaps this has grown out of their common need to protect themselves from marauding neighbors.

PUEBLO CRAFTSMEN

I haven't told you anything about specialized workers among the Pueblo Indians. There are some, particularly

silversmiths, and there are skilled potters, and individuals
good at weaving or tanning. But there are no ways of buying and selling at all. All special goods are exchanged on
an informal basis. There isn't any place at all in traditional
Pueblo living for individual accumulation of wealth.
Families who happen to have more goods than others, at
a particular time, use it up in the village ceremonies. The
highest positions and honor belong to the priests, who
have no special wealth, and live like anyone else, except
that some of their farming may be done for them when
they are busy with community tasks.

PRIESTS AND RITUAL

The priests are very important in Pueblo life. They form
a governing council for the village. They supervise the
common ceremonies. They decide when to plant and
when to harvest the corn. They plan ways to defend the

141

Pueblo from attack. They even consider individual problems when these could affect the welfare of the group: for example, someone's failure to co-operate as he should.

This important role of the priests has its roots way back among the Indians of Mexico and Central America, from whom the Pueblo Indians learned to farm. From their southern neighbors they also learned the religious customs connected with the planting and growing of grain. Some of the ceremonies were supposed to bring rain. Pueblo country is very dry, and the Rain Ceremonies became more and more important. The myths and traditions surrounding them became more and more elaborate. The men had plenty of time to devote to their religious ceremonies during the long winter months, when there were no other important jobs to be done. They could sit in their private underground clubhouses, spinning and weaving cloth and blankets; they could recite legends, and rehearse the young men in the dances.

A Pueblo priest must learn a simply enormous amount of religious poetry — days and days of it. Since there is no writing, he has to learn it all by heart, absolutely perfectly. This means that he has to start while he is still a young boy.

To be a priest, you must have a very good character. You must be neither quarrelsome nor selfish. By the time

Five healers performing curing ceremony

you are about ten years old, you have given up most of your play and are spending hours every day learning to be a priest. Already you are sober and serious and responsible. You are memorizing prayers and legends and songs. You have begun to practice making religious paintings.

The other boys get some religious training, too, but that comes when they are a little older.

Finally, all the boys have a sort of initiation into grown-up religious activity. Before this time, there has been a lot of mystery connected with the things the older people do and believe. For example, there have been great dance ceremonies in the plaza at the center of the village. The children have been given to understand that the masked dancers are really gods, the spirits of their ancestors, who have come for a feast and a happy holiday. Because they are happy, they will bring rain clouds to the Pueblos.

Only after a boy is initiated does he find out that the dancers are not gods at all — just people wearing wonderful masked costumes. The gods are supposed to dance with them, but can't actually be seen, as the children once thought. This is a rather startling thing to discover, sometimes a shocking one. Since the older people don't want the children just to feel they have been tricked (as you may have felt if you once believed in Santa Claus), they make the initiation a very important and awesome thing. For the Pueblo Indians take their religion very seriously. In it are tied up all sorts of ideas that make it possible for them to feel comfortable and to live and work together.

CO–OPERATION

Among the Bachiga people, religion had nothing at all to do with individual good and bad behavior. A man would be punished by the people he injured or cheated, not the gods. It really didn't make any important difference to the other people in his village, who weren't directly affected by his evil acts.

But Pueblo Indians take misbehavior very seriously. Everyone must co-operate, because they depend on mutual aid, and because they live in such very close quarters. For them, good behavior is very intimately tied up with religion. If people do not co-operate, if they do not play their role in ceremonies or group work, it will upset the gods and may interfere with the coming of the rains. The priests will certainly punish individuals who endanger community well-being. And religion is used also in training the children. They aren't just threatened with some punishment in an afterlife; the threat is right where they can see it. During one of their dance festivals, some of the masked figures of gods go about with whips, threatening all the children who have misbehaved in the past year. They may even make an example of one or two by whipping them. These "scare dancers" are always followed by "clown dancers," who amuse the children and give them gifts. But they have had their lesson first.

Pueblo Kachina dancer

The basic lesson in co-operation, in learning that group needs must come first, is really learned by the children in their everyday experience. Their habits of co-operation and sharing, particularly in the family, are very strong and deep. If a Pueblo child is given a piece of candy, he immediately shares it with his brothers and sisters. No child would think of trying to do better in school than other boys and girls, for fear of shaming them. What could be more rude than hurrying to finish a task before the others have finished, too? When the girls and the women work at their corn grinding, they make identical motions, keeping time, so everyone gets through at the same time.

When we look back at these two pictures of two simple farming peoples, we can add one more important idea to our understanding of them. We have seen lots of differences — in family living, in religious beliefs and ceremonies, in the way land and crops are divided. But that is not all. The people themselves have different outlooks — in their ideas of good behavior, in their regard for each other, in the things they value and work for. One is peaceful, the other ever fighting and brawling. One is co-operative, the other mistrusts even his close relatives. But in each culture, the character and habits of the people fit in with the whole way of life they have worked out, and are, indeed, part of it.

I I.

MAN THE METALWORKER

NOW you have seen something of the culture of two very different kinds of farming people, one in Africa and one in America. There were lots of others who remained primitive farmers up to modern times. Some — for example, in Oceania — combined the ways of the farmer with local trading, and with fishing. Others were different in other ways. Each had its own particular way of life, growing out of its own past, and fitting its own needs.

There were herdsmen, too. We haven't enough time now to talk about them at length; but they shared some of the farmers' advantages, and developed their own particular culture, in some ways similar, in some ways sharply different from that of the less active farmers. Perhaps someday you will read some of the books that have been written about the life ways of many of these people.

Not all of the farming and herding people remained so small and simple in their ways of living together. From what we have said you can see that as farming and sometimes herding provided man with a secure food supply, there was more opportunity for crafts to grow more complicated and specialized, for wealth to grow greater, for rulers and priests and soldiers to be supported by the labor of other people. In many parts of the world great kingdoms arose, with despotic monarchs who lived in luxury and kept great armies to maintain their power and increase their empires. The Emperor of Hawaii wore feather cloaks made of tiny red and yellow feathers from hummingbird tails. Such a cloak represented years of patient work, by workers who did not need to concern themselves with anything else. The King of Dahomey

in West Africa had hundreds of slaves who were put to death with him when he died, to make his life more comfortable in the afterworld. And not far from the Bachiga in Uganda there was a king who ruled over millions of subjects, many of them from conquered neighboring countries. All of them had to pay taxes to support the king, his wives, public officers, and a large army.

In some parts of the world, increase in wealth and power went along with a greatly increased mastery over nature. In these regions men took steps that could spread to their neighbors, and that led to the way of life we call "civilization."

In middle America, for example, men learned to work in copper and silver, and to weave wonderful tapestries. They built huge pyramids, as great as the ones in ancient Egypt. In Peru, broad stone roads ran thousands of miles along the crest of the Andes to their capital city. The Incas domesticated the llama and the alpaca, and used them for wool and as beasts of burden to carry loads. And of course, they had to be skilled organizers, too, to manage all this. Such huge projects were the work of thousands of people, who had to be fed by the work of others, who toiled in the fields, and by the tribute paid by conquered neighbors. The Inca and his family who ruled this empire were treated as gods. The Inca himself was the incarnation of

Aztec high priest

the sun, too holy to walk upon the ground; he had to be carried about in a golden palanquin. And farther to the north, in Mexico, building on many of the same foundations, the Mayas and the Aztecs in their great stone cities actually learned to write, and kept illustrated histories and religious books. They were also scientists, whose arithmetic and astronomy were more accurate and efficient than that of the ancient Romans.

In the Middle East, within a few thousand years after farming began, men began to make many new strides forward. And in this area, they were greatly aided by the fact that many different people lived near each other, so that the inventions and discoveries made by each could be pooled. This made far more rapid progress possible.

One tremendous improvement, that meant a great deal to human productivity, was the harnessing of cattle to the plow. This is one of those great inventions which seem so simple and mean such a great deal, yet actually happen so seldom in human history. It needed the combined knowledge of both farming and the raising of domesticated animals. But we know that combination wouldn't automatically produce this invention: the Bachiga and other African people do not plow their land even today! Even attempts to teach them meet with resistance, for using a plow runs directly against many of their habits, and especially against their attitude about the special value of cattle, and their prestige. To break through such a resistance, it would take some very real and recognized need — such as to produce more food.

Once animal power was put to human use in certain parts of the world, in many ways it was enormously useful. Plowing increases the amount of crops a given field can yield, and decreases the man-hours needed to work it. It frees more people for more specialized work. Great cities can grow up, fed by the produce of the countryside. And it frees men for fighting and for travel and trading. This trading and traveling was very important in the ancient

HERE ARE SOME OF THE TRADE ROUTES ALONG WHICH EARLY CIVILIZATION FLOWED

Middle East, for men were learning to work in metal, and they often depended on raw materials that had to be brought from a distance.

It was about six thousand years ago, or somewhat less, that men discovered for the first time that they could get a wonderful new substance by heating certain kinds of stones. This new substance was copper, which could be

153

smelted and worked into all sorts of forms. Within a thousand years after its discovery, the metalsmiths had learned that by adding some tin they could get a far harder and even more useful metal, which we call bronze.

This new metal craft spread rapidly among the settled farming people of the Near and Middle East. It made many differences in their lives. Tin was not found everywhere, so that trade with distant places became necessary. Trading ships and caravans went from Syria and Egypt to India and Babylon.

Bronze was valuable, and the rulers who controlled it grew rich and powerful. Writing and coining money were developed to meet the needs of complicated trading and government. Within a few thousand years after farming itself had begun, great civilizations, all fed by the same streams of progress and invention, had developed in Egypt, in Asia Minor and in India. Later this way of life spread still further, to China and to Crete. All of these people shared a great deal of knowledge and culture, but each was also different in many ways, because each had different particular circumstances to cope with and different previous ways of living.

The art of working metals spread slowly up into Europe. Traders from the south exchanged implements and tools of bronze for raw materials, such as skins and amber.

As time passed, the northern people of Europe learned to make bronze themselves, and they developed tools and weapons more exactly suited to their needs.

But by that time men had also learned to work in iron. Iron was cheaper and easier to get than bronze. It could make tools for every man instead of just for the wealthy few. People could have plows and axes, instead of just ornaments for the rulers and weapons for their soldiers. This meant that the conditions under which civilization came to Europe were somewhat different from those which built the lavish despotic empires of the East.

This is the background out of which our civilization grew. We are not going to look at the rest of it in detail, for we are now entering the borders of recorded history, and that is another book.

Looking at this background which we have been surveying, you now realize that the civilization of which we are a part is not our own special creation. It was built by many peoples, upon foundations laid by many others. The Phoenicians developed the alphabet we use. The Arabs worked out our system of writing numbers and doing calculations. The gunpowder that helped Europeans conquer the New World came originally from China. Many of our foods came from the Indians, and others from Central Asia. Muslin and calico came from India, and silk from China.

Even our language comes from many different sources. And to understand our true indebtedness, we have to go back even further — to the first men who learned to farm, to the men of the Stone and Bronze and Iron Ages who worked out in crude form all the fundamental tools of our basic tool kit.

Just imagine making any of our complex modern gadgets or machines if such a simple thing as a nail had not been worked out ages ago by other men! Suppose you first had to design and invent your tools and materials and even such basic things as hammers and saws, bolts and pulleys and levers?

You can understand why man's first steps were such long, slow, difficult ones, and why many people of the world, with so much less shared knowledge to build on, could add so much less to the total of human knowledge. Just compare Robert Fulton with a Melanesian fisherman. Each wanted to make a better kind of boat. Robert Fulton

invented the paddle-wheel steamboat. The Melanesian invented only an outrigger for his canoe. Fulton wanted to increase the *speed* of ships, because he lived at a time when Americans were competing furiously with each other for trade with foreign countries. He made his steamboat by combining various kinds of knowledge — wheels, steam engines, the properties of metal, and so on.

The Melanesian was also driven by trading needs, but of a different sort. His main problem was increased *safety,* so his frail canoes could sail to distant islands with their loads. He too used what knowledge he had — knowledge of sailing and of how to fasten things by lashing them with handmade rope. He devised a floating extension to the canoe which kept it from tipping over without increasing its weight too much or making it difficult to handle. The float is shaped something like the canoe itself, only it is smaller. It is lashed to the canoe by long poles, so that it floats parallel to the canoe, some feet away. The poles can be covered with a platform to hold loads. This device broadens the base of the canoe so that it is less likely to tip.

Fulton and the Melanesian fisherman had quite the same kind of interest in experiments. Both paid attention to details and stuck at the job they wanted to do. But they were facing different needs, and they had altogether different bodies of knowledge available.

We have been able to share in the major tides of human progress, and so to build our civilization. But that doesn't mean we are any better or cleverer than other people. It doesn't mean we are cleaner or more polite, either!

When the anthropologist says "civilized" he uses the word in a special technical sense. He means people who keep written records and carry on business with their neighbors near and far. He means people who live in cities, and get their food from farmers outside the city limits. He means that there are lots of specialized workers, and at least the beginnings of modern science.

You have seen that with the growth of technical complexity man's ways of living and working together have also grown and changed. Some of the conditions of modern social living have no counterpart at all in the primitive world.

But nevertheless they also have their roots in that world.

Our social living, like our technology, has grown up over the ages. It is based on the life ways of our own particular ancestors. Some of those ways were similar to, some different from those of the particular people we have been studying in this book. Studying them, we learn to look at our culture for what it is — not a way of life ideally suited to our needs, but one which grew up in piecemeal fashion out of older ways. It is not a natural, permanent and necessary human way of behaving, but a way man has fashioned for himself, which he is constantly changing.

I2.

DOES "RACE" MAKE A DIFFERENCE?

WE'VE been talking about all sorts
of clues to the differences between people, but there's one
obvious difference that we haven't even mentioned. We
have paid no attention at all to the way people *look*. Certainly the Eskimos with their ivory-colored skins look different from the very dark Bachiga. The heavy-browed
Australian Bushmen look different from the high-cheeked
Pueblo Indians. And all of them are different from most
European-Americans.

Aren't these things clues that we should follow? Un-
doubtedly you have heard it said that dark skin color, for
example, is a sign, even an explanation, of some people's
backwardness. Is this true?

Some of us may take it for granted that the answer to
these questions is "Yes." But anthropologists don't. They
have examined these questions scientifically, and their
answer is a definite "No."

160

Some people think it ought to be possible to put this question to a very simple test. Why not just give the different peoples of the world intelligence tests, such as you probably have taken in school? Measure their IQ's and find out if they are equal. But that just isn't possible. Let's take an actual example and see why.

Suppose you were one of the Australian Bushmen, say a child of the Arunta tribe. Suppose someone tried to give you the kind of intelligence test that American boys and girls take. You couldn't possibly answer the questions on it: "What would you do if you were on the way to school and realized you were going to be late?" After all, you've never seen a school or a clock in your life! Nor could you complete a picture of an automobile drawn without a steering wheel. You've never had a ride in an automobile.

You'd surely do badly on such a test, no matter how clever you were.

But what about simple arithmetic problems? Most children learn to add and subtract by the time they are eight or nine. Couldn't we give those to you? Well, here again you would fail. You wouldn't know anything about arithmetic. Not because you were stupid, but for the simple reason that you'd never in your life had to calculate anything. In fact, the Arunta people seldom even need to *count* anything — or have anything to count!

You certainly would fail in an American intelligence test if you were an Arunta child.

Now suppose things were turned around. You are yourself again and an Arunta is trying to find out how clever you are. Suppose he shows you some footprints on the ground and says, "Here are animal tracks. Tell me what kind of animal made them. Then follow the tracks and bring back the game."

To him, that kind of problem is as simple as two times two. He can recognize individual footprints, not only of animals but of people as well. He can follow a trail where you and I would swear nobody had walked. He can even tell individuals apart by their tracks.

Could you pass a test in remembering footprints instead of numbers?

A scientist once worked out some tests which he believed would really tell him something about native Australians. And then he ran into another difficulty. He had a very hard time persuading anyone to try the tests. They thought the whole thing was silly. They aren't used to our idea of individual competition — it has no place in their lives. They just couldn't see why it mattered who got the answer first, working alone, when obviously if they worked together they could solve the problem faster.

162

However, the scientist was persistent, and he found that the Australian Bushmen did remarkably well on a test in which they had to solve the problem of getting out of a maze.

You have probably solved maze problems for fun. How does it happen that Bushmen solve them well, too? Remember that they are expert trackers. A maze problem makes sense to them, because it is not so very different from the problem of tracking.

The fact is that intelligence and skill are found among all people. Not only that, every culture and every way of life makes high demands upon its members. But intelligence and skill develop differently in different cultures. *They develop in ways which meet people's needs.*

Bushmen have to be clever about tracking in order to eat at all. American boys and girls, no matter what the color of their skin, have to learn about the things that are important in *their* lives. For example, we learn to do hard arithmetic problems because arithmetic is important: we must be able to count our money and measure the things we buy and sell. We have to do more complicated mathematics before we can work with radio, electricity, airplanes and all modern inventions.

Other peoples know a lot about the things that they

have to deal with. Skill and intelligence are not the monopoly of tall or short people, light ones or dark. Looks have nothing to do with it.

We've already seen that people of every sort have made inventions. Our own progress is built on these inventions borrowed from many, many peoples. Our civilization was built by contributions from people of all colors, and people from all parts of the world are still making contributions today.

If we look back through history, we find that at different times different groups have led all the others in civilization. Once it was the dark-skinned Egyptians who were far ahead in producing the things that mankind needed and in organizing a complicated way of life. At another time it was the fairer-skinned Greeks. Later the Romans forged ahead. At that time, the light-skinned people of Northern Europe, who are in the forefront in modern times, were barbarians. The people of the land we now call England had no writing, and no true cities. They painted their faces blue when they went to war. Do you know what the Roman writer Cicero thought of these backward people? This is what he wrote to a friend: "I must advise you never to take one of these British slaves into your home to be a house servant. They are not fitted

for such work, since they are not capable of civilization."

Of course, Britons soon proved that they were "capable
of civilization." And so are all other people.

Here is a true story that sums up what anthropologists
have discovered about differences in intelligence and skill
among people whose way of life is different and who
happen to be different in skin-color. It is told by Ellsworth
Faris in his book *The Nature of Human Nature*. Mr. Faris
is a famous sociologist who lived for a number of years in
the Belgian Congo. He was talking to a native, he tells us,
and pointed out to him that less than a thousand Belgians
were able to rule twenty million Congo natives. The reply
was immediate.

"Give us breech-loading guns and ammunition, and
within a month there will not be one of the thousand left
alive here," said the native.

"But," said the white man, "that is the point. The white
men invented and made their guns and ammunition."

"Sir, do you know how to make a gun and ammunition?"

"Well, no — not yet — but I could learn to make them
in a factory," the sociologist answered.

"Certainly you could, if they would teach you." The
native clinched the argument. "But so could we."

165

CULTURE IS NOT IN OUR BLOOD

Let's look at it another way: Changes in civilization
don't depend on changes in people. People can change
their whole way of life completely because of historical
events. This doesn't change the color of their skin or the
shape of their noses. The Plains Indians in this country
were farmers when Columbus crossed the Atlantic. But
after the Spaniards brought horses to America, these
people took to riding. Many of them, as you know, then
gave up farming altogether. They became buffalo hunters.

The same sort of thing happened to the Japanese. They
look today as they looked one hundred years ago, before
they opened their country to American ships and trade.
But their way of living has certainly changed, and so have
the things in which they are skilled.

Because human culture is learned by each generation, and does not just pass on through the bloodstream, normal human babies from anywhere can learn to take their place in any culture. What individuals do and how they behave depend upon how they were brought up, not upon the color of their skins.

Suppose you had been adopted by an Arunta family when you were a tiny baby. You, too, would believe that working in a group is more important than working alone. You would think it silly to compete with others in tests. You, too, would be ignorant of arithmetic, but good at tracking. Perhaps you might even be an expert in your group. And just the opposite happens to all the babies brought up in our culture. Through education and experience, they learn our ways, no matter how different from those in the land their parents came from.

This doesn't mean that no individual can change later on. Quite the opposite is true. People who have grown up in one culture can learn to get along in other cultures too, if they need to. And again it doesn't matter at all whether their color matches or is different. The explorer Stefansson lived among the Eskimos and adopted their ways of surviving in the cold North. The pioneers on the frontier in this country had to master the Indians' skills in order to survive. Today there are United Nations representatives who grew up in backward villages, in various parts of the world, and later graduated from big modern universities. One of the Area Representatives comes from the tribe right next to the Bachiga in East Africa.

Sometimes circumstances have made the change very difficult. When the people of Africa were brought over here as slaves, they were certainly not in a position to learn about and take part in the best accomplishments of our civilization. In fact, they were often carefully kept from even learning how to read. Nonetheless, even in slavery times, leaders arose among the slaves, men and women like Harriet Tubman and Frederick Douglass, who have taken their place among the great Americans of all time.

TALENT

Of course, not everyone develops into a great genius. Special abilities differ among individuals. In your own class in school there are certainly some children who are better than others with their hands, who draw well, or make wonderful airplane models. Others are excellent athletes, while some do particularly well in their studies — better perhaps in some subjects than in others. You certainly wouldn't expect to tell by the color of a child's hair or the shape of his nose which of these special abilities he had. You know perfectly well that blondes aren't really any dumber — or any smarter — than brunettes. It isn't even true that big heads or high foreheads go with lofty thoughts.

And just as you can't tell by his appearance how bright, or how good a singer, some child may be — so anthropologists and psychologists know we can't tell such things for whole groups of people, either. There are individuals with special talents among all peoples; no talent is the special property of any particular group.

Perhaps you have heard that Negroes are especially musical. If this were so, then musical ability should belong to Negroes generally, not just to some particular ones — not just to Marian Anderson, but to my Bachiga friends as well. Although some among the Bachiga were gifted musically, most of them were as scratchy-voiced as I. They had no orchestras. Few of them could play any sort of instrument. The Negro people of West Africa have a wealth of songs to accompany every kind of activity. Not so my Bachiga friends. Their only rhythmic work songs were paddling songs, sung by the various clans whose homes bordered the lake. Otherwise, they usually sang only at dances.

There are individuals with every kind of gift among the people of any group or culture. Sometimes a particular

169

kind of talent will fit in very well with a people's way of life. Then individuals who have that kind of talent will flourish, and their special skill will be richly developed. But if there is nothing in their culture to develop these particular gifts, they will lie dormant — asleep. For example, in Samoa, they don't sing melodies as we do. Their songs only have different rhythmic patterns. But missionaries can teach young Samoan children to sing hymns with melodies just as well as we do.

The same goes for every other kind of special ability we know about, and for special physical gifts and defects, too. Singers with beautiful voices, swift runners, albinos with no color in their skin or eyes or hair — some of these are found among all peoples in all parts of the world.

ALL MEN ARE BROTHERS

Many people think of mankind as divided into clear-cut, sharply distinct groups. And they expect these groups to be very different in character and ability as well as in physical appearance.

But to anthropologists it has been obvious for some time that mankind is not divided into clear-cut, sharply distinct groups. Most human traits, even physical traits, are shared among all people; all men belong to the same human family. The color of people's eyes may be a little different, but the nerves and muscles of the eyes are always connected with the brain and the skull in the same way. In fact, it is possible to transplant an eye from one man to another so that the eye will live and grow and *see*. And it doesn't make the least bit of difference what parts of the world the two men come from!

Even the Nazi doctors knew that they could study the human body by experimenting on Jewish people in concentration camps, although their propaganda said that Jews were less than human. When a medical student learns how the body of one man works, he knows about the bodies of all men all over the world. A doctor can tell from a tooth or two, a heart or lung or skull, whether he is looking at part of a human body or a part of some other animal. But not even the greatest expert can tell from any of the parts what color a man's skin was. He cannot tell the brain of a Negro from that of a white man.

Of course, there *are* differences between people. Some have large noses, others small ones. Some have dark hair, others are blond. But most of these differences are scattered among all the different people of the world. Take height, for example. Being very tall isn't the special property of any one people in the world. The Highland Scotch are very tall, and so are some of the Plains Indians. The very tallest people live in Central Africa — the famous "giant" Watussi you may have seen in the movies. But not *all* the people of any such group are equally tall. And right among us, there are some individuals tall enough to pass muster even among the Watussi. In fact there may be very tall and very short individuals right in the same family.

There is one difference between people that is very striking indeed, though you can't see it. That is the difference in their types of blood.

If you've ever been in a hospital for an operation, you know that the doctor orders a test to find out which of several groups your blood belongs to. Then, if you need a transfusion, he will know what type of blood to use. (In a transfusion, a small quantity of someone else's blood is actually dripped through a tube into your veins. Doctors have found that transfusions help people after an accident or an operation.)

Using the right type of blood is very important. Some kinds of blood are so different that mixing them could cause death. Now the interesting thing is this: you can't judge blood type by appearance or even relationship. Your own brother's blood might kill you, but blood from individuals in Asia or Africa may be exactly like yours!

172

Not all differences between people are scattered so widely over the world. Some traits are concentrated to some extent in different areas, so that it is possible to tell a Chinese from a Central African, a Melanesian from a Scandinavian, and so on.

The people of Europe are light-skinned and very hairy. Some of them are blond, and they tend to have wavy hair.

People of Africa and Melanesia have dark skins and very tightly curled hair. Some of them have full lips and rather wide noses.

American Indians and the people of Eastern Asia have very straight hair indeed, and little hair on their faces or bodies.

There are others, too, all distinctive enough on the whole in their combinations of characteristic traits so we can pretty easily identify them.

Polynesian   *Filipino*   *Ainu*

Until quite recently, these different populations were treated as "races," which were considered quite separate and distinct. People had different ways of dividing them up. One of the most popular was according to "color": you may have read in some geography books that there were five different races, black, white, brown, yellow and red. (In point of fact, these particular distinctions don't really fit anybody. No one is really black or white. We are all varying shades of brown, with a little more or less of a few basic pigments.)

However they were divided up, the different "races" were once supposed to be sharply different from each other. The differences were believed to go clear back to the beginning of man's existence on earth. Any confusions were presumably due to modern crisscrossings and mixtures, which had disturbed an older simpler order.

But the anthropologist today is not satisfied with such an account. He is not content with a rough impression of the "type" to be found in any area. He insists on making measurements, on actual counting and testing. And then he finds that the old view simply does not fit the facts.

According to the old view, dark skin and kinky hair were supposed to be "racial" traits that went together. But if you look at these pictures, you will see that they don't always go together.

This South African Bushman with his sandy skin has the kinkiest hair of all.

This dark young Hindu is classed as "white" even by the old geography books, because his other features, including his wavy hair, are so European.

The native Australians are sometimes called "blackfellows" because they are so dark, but they have long wavy hair and beards.

And facial traits don't correspond neatly with either of these other traits.

This is not a modern movie actor. It is the profile of a native of Melanesia.

This gentleman is a characteristic East Coast African.

Who says Europeans are "big-noses"? This is the famous Dakota warrior, whose picture is on our nickels. He has the long straight hair and smooth skin of his Asiatic cousins, but neither the flat nose nor almond eyes that many of them have. His looks are characteristic of the Plains Sioux.

176

These two men are both Swedish. One of them you would recognize as such very easily. We might think of him as "typical," with his blond hair, rugged build and features. The other doesn't look Scandinavian at all. But there are about as many of him in Sweden as there are of the other: which is few in each case. Most Scandinavians are like neither of these. They have some of the "typical" traits, but not all.

ALL PEOPLES CHANGE

Now you see why the anthropologist does not consider the old ideas about the "races of mankind" scientifically accurate. He has found that there are no large populations that he can point to and say, "This group is pure and distinct, different from other varieties of mankind in a number of clear-cut ways."

There are at least three different factors that make for the differences we find between people. One of these is easy to understand. Men just haven't ever stayed put. For ages and ages, since long before written history, they have moved about. Sometimes they migrated in large groups from one place to another, sometimes in small groups. And wherever different groups have met they have inter-married.

Again and again, through thousands of years, invaders from Asia have swept into Europe. The countries around the Mediterranean Sea have always been blending places for people from Africa, Europe and Asia. The great ancient civilizations in Egypt, Persia, Greece and Rome were melting pots quite as much as modern America. In fact, they were even more so, because marriage between men and women of different groups was more usual. Although northern Europe was more isolated, mingling went on even there. A proud part of Viking life was the regular raids on other regions. In these raids on southern Europe, North Africa and other lands, women were captured, and they were among the mothers of later generations in the northland. So any idea that there is such a thing as a pure

"Nordic" group descended from the Vikings is simply a myth. And the same sort of things were happening in other parts of the world, whose history is less familiar to us.

When populations mingle in this way, they make quite new combinations of their various traits. That is because inheritance is a piecemeal affair. We don't look exactly like our mothers or our fathers. I may inherit some traits from my mother's side of the family, some from my father's. Putting it a little more simply than it actually is, I may have my mother's red hair, my father's classical profile, and curly hair like my grandmother. And so I have a brand-new combination of traits that may not have gone together in *any* of my ancestors.

When populations with different traits mingle, the same kind of thing happens. The characteristic traits may be reshuffled to make quite new "typical" combinations.

INHERITANCE CHANGES

Another thing that makes people different is this. The traits that we inherit are handed down through the action of tiny particles in our bodies. Biologists call these *genes*. Genes are handed down from parent to child. But they do not remain absolutely unchanged forever. From time to time they change somewhat. (Biologists call these changes that take place in a gene *mutations*.) When a gene changes, there are changes in the plant or animal of which it is part — changes that we can see, such as the color or shape of various parts. For example, in fruit flies (about whose genes we know the most) there are gene mutations which appear from time to time and change the color of the eyes, the number of bristles, the length of the wings, and so on. These mutations are inherited, and passed along from parent to child until they in their turn change.

Mutations have been going on in man all the time, just as they have in all living things. And mutations are still going on today. We can't assume that any traits we find in a group are part of a very ancient heritage. They may instead be new developments. The blondness common in northern Europe, for example, may not mean that the people are all descended from blond ancestors. It may be a more recent trait, which could have spread there because it was useful in such a climate. You probably know that one of the important vitamins — vitamin D — is made in our bodies through the action of sunlight on cells underneath our skin. Dark-colored skins do not allow sunlight to go through so readily. In Europe, where there is not much sun, it is possible that those people who had lighter skins could produce more vitamin D, and so were healthier; their lighter-skinned children were healthier and could survive better. Where there is too much sun, on the other hand, darker skin helps to screen out some of the excessive ultraviolet rays.

So the fact that Europeans are light-skinned needn't mean that they are all direct descendants of an ancient special light branch of mankind. Their ancient ancestry may even be very mixed, and their modern resemblances something achieved more recently.

ENVIRONMENT MAKES A DIFFERENCE

Besides mutations and the mingling of different groups, there is one other thing that makes for change. Even when people have much the same inheritance, there may be differences between individuals who grow up in different surroundings. Biologists have been able to give us some startling examples of this among animals and plants. For example, if they put embryo salamanders in a refrigerator for a few hours, the creatures will grow up to have only one eye, instead of two, like their brothers and sisters.

We know that whole generations of people grow up stunted after devastating ways or famines. And living conditions in this rich country have been producing taller and taller people all the time.

Change and variety — these are the ancient heritage of man. There is no time in human history that we can point to and say, based on facts: "Then, at least, groups were stable and uniform and each neatly different from the other."

PEOPLES AND RACES

Now you can see why anthropologists don't like to use the term "race."

The word "race" has a definite scientific meaning. It means a breed of animals or plants which is distinct from the rest of its species, like Angora cats or Shetland ponies. Races may be different from each other in one or more genes. This difference is kept up because one race is cut off from the rest of its species by some barrier which keeps it from mingling and pooling its genes with the rest of its kind. The barrier is usually geographical. North American forms of many animals are different in one or two traits from their European or Asiatic cousins of the same species. In domestic animals it is the breeder's selection which keeps races of dogs or cows or horses apart. You can see that there just aren't any human groups of any size which fit this picture, although it might fit some tiny isolated populations.

182

Anthropologists believe, in fact, that "race" is an unfortunate word altogether, full of fuzzy meanings and prejudice. People often say "race" where they mean a nation, like the British, who have been enormously mixed even in recent times. People even use "race" when they mean religious groups, such as Jews, or people that speak one language, like "Latins." Now, anybody can learn any language or religion. You cannot sensibly refer to a Jewish race, once you know that there are Chinese and African Jews, and that they look like the people of China and Africa, not like Syrians or East Europeans or Spaniards as the Jewish people of these regions do.

Most important of all, there obviously isn't any sense at all in the notion of "higher" and "lower," "superior" and "inferior" races. All men are brothers, descended from mixed common ancestry.

Not so long ago, the Nazis in Germany developed the theory that the colored people of the world were closer to the apes than the "superior" white Aryans. They even divided the Aryans into groups, with themselves at the top —a specially gifted group whom they called Nordics. They talked about Nordics as though they were rugged blonds. But only a small number of Germans actually are blond. Certainly Hitler himself was neither blond nor rugged.

In this country, before the Civil War, slave owners built up a similar theory that Negroes were not really human; that they were a separate kind of creature, different from true mankind. They used all kinds of arguments, trying to justify one man's owning another in a country that was supposed to be democratic. If Negroes were human, then it was against American principles to keep them slaves. But if they were not human, then everybody's conscience could be clear. So they even tried to use quotations from the Bible to prove that Negroes were different, and that they didn't have "souls."

There are people in America today who still believe that some groups are more "apelike" than others. And plenty of people feel that others are very strange and distasteful if they have a different skin color or different nose — or even different religions or languages.

Naturally, when a large group of people have a feeling as strong as this, they behave badly to the others. Their false and unscientific ideas are taught to children, and so prejudice and bad behavior can become part of a people's culture. These false ideas can cut very deep. A psychologist once asked children to look at a picture of people in a library. Afterwards he asked them, "What was the Negro man doing?" Lots and lots of children answered, "He was sweeping." This was not true at all. But it fitted the children's ideas of what would be appropriate. Their prejudice actually twisted their impression of what they saw!

A great deal of bitterness and pain is caused by deep prejudices such as these. And it is obvious that such ideas don't fit the facts at all. Now that we are beginning to live in one world where it is easy for people from all over the globe to be in touch with each other, it is very important that we all know this. We must know the scientific facts, and not let prejudice influence our dealings with the many different peoples of the world. No human groups are "higher" or "lower" than any others. None are pure races, different and distinct from all others. People of different color may be more like you in many other traits than members of your own family.

All the different kinds of people we find in the world today, dark-skinned and light, smooth and curly-haired, tall and short, are one order of being, fruits of one family tree. All are equally remote from our distant subhuman ancestors whom we all left behind perhaps a million years ago. Differences in their behavior are cultural. These differences are not in people's genes, but in the way they grew up, in the accumulated knowledge and experience available to them. Given the opportunity, all of mankind, no matter what their looks, are equally "capable of civilization."

13.
CONCLUSION

Now we have met briefly a few of the peoples of the earth. Perhaps from their stories you can guess how amazingly rich and wonderful the possibilities of mankind are — and how exciting is the work of understanding people in all their variations, of finding out how all of mankind lives; how our present ways of behaving came into being and how they may change.

The same things we have said about learning to understand those who seem strange to us apply to ourselves as well. We must ask the same questions about our own ways of life as we do about Eskimos or Australians or Africans. How do we actually behave? How do the different parts of our culture fit together? What do we cherish and strive for, and how do we learn to value these things? This is something that anthropologists are just beginning to do. Working with other scientists, they are trying to get a true

186

picture of our own culture. They want us to study ourselves just as scientifically and critically as we study others.

And they want us to treat others with the dignity and
decency that comes of understanding them, and their differences from us. We have seen that our civilization has
grown from contributions made by many different people.
If we can all learn to work together, we can hope to build
a far greater civilization in the future — a rich and varied
civilization, based on the pooled contributions of all mankind.

SOME OTHER BOOKS

Linton, Ralph and Adelin	*Man's Way: From Cave to Skyscraper*
Eberle, Irmengarde	*Big Family of Peoples*
Ilin, M., and Segal, F.	*How Man Became a Giant*
	Giant at the Crossroads
Van Loon, Henrik Willem	*Ancient Man*
White, Alice Terry	*Prehistoric America*

Some books, though written for younger readers, are accurate and very interesting:

Evans, Eva Knox	*All About Us*
	People Are Important
Hogben, Lancelot T.	*How the First Men Lived*
	The First Great Inventions

There are lots of interesting books that deal accurately with Eskimos and American Indians, including:

Holling, Holling C.	*Book of Indians*
Brindze, Ruth	*Story of the Totem Pole*
Bleeker, Sonia	*Indians of the Longhouse*
	Raiders of the South West

Many books written as exciting stories give a good picture of real life. Among them are:

Freuchen, Pipaluk	*Eskimo Boy*
Gray Owl	*Sajo and the Beaver People*
Moon, Grace	*Daughter of Thunder*
Means, Florence C.	*Whispering Girl*

It's harder to find books for other parts of the world that give a good picture of the life of the native peoples. Here are a few good stories that some libraries have:

Best, Herbert	*Garram the Hunter*
Gatti, Emilio	*Saranga, the Pygmy*
Singer, Caroline, and Baldridge, Cyrus L.	*Boomba Lives in Africa*
Stevens, A. J.	*Lion Boy*
Enright, Elizabeth	*Kintu, a Congo Adventure*
Elliott, Kathleen M.	*Soomoon, Boy of Bali*
	Riema, Little Brown Girl of Java
Morgan, De Wolfe	*Messenger to the Pharaoh*
Dragonet, Edward	*Saltar the Mongol*

INDEX

191

192

194

South Africans, 49, 77; appearance, 175, inventions, 68
South America, 47, 150
Spirits, Ba, 26, 126–130; Es, 59–63; Pu, 144
Stefansson, V., 62, 97
Stevenson, R. L., 34
Stone tools, 37–44, 72, 80, 98
Stories, Es, 14
Stream of knowledge, 49

Talent, 168–170
Tobacco, 88
Tools, for farming, 87–89; see also Inventions
Totem, 77
Totem pole, 79, 82
Trading, 100, 152–155; Ba, 103–107; Pu, 141
Tug of war, Es, 55
Turkeys, 96

Uncle, position of, 137–138

Villages, Au, 72–73; Ba, 24; Es, 50–51; NW, 81–82; Pu, 132–134, 140; farming, 99

War, 113; Ba feuds and, 112–113; Es attitude toward, 53–55
Wealth, 150; of hunters, 68; Ba, 123–125, 131; Es, 56; NW, 84; Pu, 142
Weaving, 99; Pu, 136
Wedding, Ba, 119–121
Wheat, 86–87
Women, and farming, 91–92; Au, 70–71, 76; Ba, 108–110; position of, 135–139; Pu, 137
Writing, 154, 158